Blessed Are You

....

FINDING INSPIRATION
from
OUR SISTERS
in
FAITH

....

Melanie Rigney

Franciscan
MEDIA
Cincinnati, Ohio

Scripture passages have been taken from *New Revised Standard Version Bible,* copyright ©1989 by the Division of Christian Education of the National Council of the Churches of Christ in the U.S.A., and used by permission. All rights reserved. Quotes from Pope Francis, Pope Benedict XVI, and Pope John Paul II as well as the English translation of the *Catechism of the Catholic Church* for the United States of America (indicated as CCC), 2nd ed. Copyright 1997 by United States Catholic Conference—Libreria Editrice Vaticana, are used by permission. All rights reserved.

Cover design by Mary Ann Smith
Cover image © Shutterstock | Syda Productions
Book design by Mark Sullivan

LIBRARY OF CONGRESS CATALOGING-IN-PUBLICATION DATA
Rigney, Melanie.
Blessed are you : finding inspiration from our sisters in faith / Melanie Rigney.
pages cm
Includes bibliographical references.
ISBN 978-1-61636-880-7 (alk. paper)
1. Catholic women—Religious life. 2. Beatitudes—Criticism, interpretation, etc. 3. Christian women saints—Biography 4. Catholic women—Biography. I. Title.
BX2353.R534 2015
282.092'52—dc23
2015012147

ISBN 978-1-61636-880-7
Published by Franciscan Media
28 W. Liberty St.
Cincinnati, OH 45202
www.FranciscanMedia.org

Printed in the United States of America.
Printed on acid-free paper.
15 16 17 18 19   5 4 3 2 1

To Adrienne, Ann, Anne, Anne Marie, Annie, Cathy, Colleen,
Duffy, Elaine, Fran, Helene, Henri, Karen, Kathy, Laura, Leslie,
Margie, Marylee, Meg, Nora, Sandy…
and all churchwomen of any age.
Blessed are you, indeed.

When Jesus saw the crowds, he went up the mountain; and after he sat down, his disciples came to him. Then he began to speak, and taught them, saying:

"Blessed are the poor in spirit, for theirs is the kingdom of heaven.

"Blessed are those who mourn, for they will be comforted.

"Blessed are the meek, for they will inherit the earth.

"Blessed are those who hunger and thirst for righteousness, for they will be filled.

"Blessed are the merciful, for they will receive mercy.

"Blessed are the pure in heart, for they will see God.

"Blessed are the peacemakers, for they will be called children of God.

"Blessed are those who are persecuted for righteousness' sake, for theirs is the kingdom of heaven.

"Blessed are you when people revile you and persecute you and utter all kinds of evil against you falsely on my account. Rejoice and be glad, for your reward is great in heaven, for in the same way they persecuted the prophets who were before you."

—MATTHEW 5:1–12

contents

Supreme blessedness.

Couldn't we all use *more* of *that?*

Supreme blessedness, or happiness, is the definition of *beatitude.*

This book helps us discover and explore beatitude, and more precisely, how we might come to *live* this blessedness. In it, you'll encounter Melanie Rigney's deft and dynamic pairings of the paradoxical words of Jesus Christ in the Beatitudes, with the wisdom she's sifted from the lives of saintly women.

I'm fortunate to know many good women, faithful women. Faith in Jesus is a compass offering direction and purpose for their lives. Their influence on my life has been transformative. It's no cliché to say that these women *bless* me, and inspire me to live better. These friends not only inspire, they accompany me. They are my prayerful supporters when I'm in need, my go-to gals when it's time to celebrate, and my boon companions serving alongside me when something must be done. Their company brings sweet comfort. Most important, they are my true sisters in Christ. They cheer me on toward heaven—the goal of all beatitude—that I may one day to meet Jesus face to face.

Yet there's an unseen cohort in my life, too. The communion of saints is real. And the women of heaven, who once trod the earth we walk today, have a worthy sisterhood to pass on to us. The book you are holding is an encouragement for you and me to widen the circle of the women *we* hold dear, and, to better know the saintly women who hold *us* dear. Their life stories offer hope that we might strengthen our attitudes, habits, and virtues, in the ways of grace.

The Beatitudes remind us of the necessary *attitudes* we must possess in order to *be* active Christians. The Beatitudes shape and form us, like *be attitudes*, to live in the way that Jesus desires us to *be*...to be more like him...to *be blessed*...to *be more* than minimalists or skimmers of the surface of life...to *become* deep divers into beatitude.

How often have the words or deeds of a good friend been the face of Jesus to me? Many times. Perhaps that has been your experience too. But even if this is a new idea for you, I invite you to seek a greater knowledge of the saintly women you'll find in this book. The saints are friends waiting to meet us—sisters who want us to know Jesus, and to experience a transforming love through a living, committed, faith.

We often hear it said that friends are the family that we choose for ourselves. If so, let us choose the friends of Jesus to be among our own. The best of friends always call one another higher, in imitation of the Divine Friend, Jesus.

The *Catechism of the Catholic Church* declares: "The Beatitudes depict the countenance of Jesus Christ and portray his charity."

To live the Beatitudes is to *be* like Jesus, to reflect his countenance, and to *be* his charity in the world. Picture Jesus's face, and his example, in each of the Beatitudes as you read them in *Blessed are You*. The real blessing will come when you can picture your own face, and your faithful example, following Jesus! It's challenging, yet rewarding. What Melanie Rigney has done in this book is demonstrate the powerful countenance of Jesus that comes through the faces of faith-filled women, chapter by chapter, beatitude by beatitude. So take notes on the women who inspire *you.*

More than famous list of proverbs, the Beatitudes are paradoxical promises—hope in the midst of tribulation—and a response to the holy desire for happiness that God has placed within our hearts. Memorize them and make them your own.

I first met Melanie Rigney in the pages of her book, *Sisterhood of Saints.* That title suggests the kinship Christians share with the saints in heaven. Melanie continues to explore those positive connections in *Blessed Are You.* She is an able researcher, and a perceptive chronicler of the lives of the saints.

Melanie and I eventually met in person when I interviewed her for my podcast, *Among Women.* We enjoyed a wonderful meal and conversation on the Florida coast as we both attended an event for the National Council of Catholic Women. How happy are we to share a sisterhood in the family of God, and in the writing world.

Today, Melanie remains an intercessor who prays for me. I'm sure she is praying for you, and all who read this book.

May this book help us come to know our supreme blessedness. May we also encounter new sisters in Christ within the communion of the saints who cannot wait to meet us, one fine day, in that *eternal beatitude,* together with Jesus.

—Pat Gohn, author, *Blessed, Beautiful, and Bodacious:*
Celebrating the Gift of Catholic Womanhood

The Beatitudes.

Doesn't it just make you smile to say that out loud, to think of Jesus going up that mountain, sitting down, and then speaking those beautiful words?

The challenge is that to Jesus and therefore to us, the Beatitudes are more than words. They are a way to follow him. They lay out an exceedingly difficult road map to live. Be meek? Me? Be a peacemaker? Me? Find something positive in mourning? Me? Yes, you. And all of us.

I often speak about the female saints to Catholic women's groups, and two things tug at my heart. The first is the little boxes we try to put these holy women in. They weren't perfect, folks, and they would have been the first to tell you about their struggles with the loss of loved ones, their health, their dignity. The faith and confidence they had in the Lord make them bigger than those little boxes. That brings us to the second thing: Like them, you are blessed. Not tomorrow, not when the kids go off to college, not when you get that next promotion. Now. Today. How do I know that? Because Jesus told us. Note the Beatitudes are not in the future tense, or the past, for that matter. You are blessed *now*, today and always, just like the women on these pages. Believe it.

The blessings abound, whenever two or more are gathered in his name. And as women, we are great at gathering, aren't we?

Let me give you an example. A couple of years ago, a dear friend who's a bit older was confined to her home for weeks at a time. She's been a widow for many years, and some of her children live quite a distance away. Still, there was never any frenzy about who was bringing dinner what night or who was taking her to the doctor which morning. Her longtime friends—the Ladies of the Church—had it covered via phone, e-mail and intuition.

The Ladies of the Church have met for decades. If I recall correctly, they started as a babysitting co-op and then morphed into so much more. They write crazy songs to sing at one another's birthdays, weddings, and retirements. They pray together. They laugh together. They cry together. They love one another deeply. They are Christ to one another.

One day, my friend Karen and I were talking about how much we both admire this woman—and about how we wanted a Ladies of the Church group of our own, but one that is a little different. We agreed we'd both like to be part of a group in which women about our ages support one another in living our faith lives and, indeed, every aspect of our lives with meaning and purpose through Christ. Our families and people through our parishes or other faith groups take us to doctors' appointments and bring us meals when we're sick, and we appreciate that. But sisterhood is different. Sisterhood is unique. Sisterhood is holy.

The answer we received from Christ was to form our own group. We call it Churchwomen of a Certain Age. The general idea is that you need to be between fifty and sixty-five (though we've allowed a young'un or two in) and not to get stressed if you can't make all or even any of the gatherings. We try to get together quarterly. Sometimes we do that more often; sometimes, less often.

Generally, the gatherings are a potluck and sharing at someone's home; we've also gone to a theatrical version of *Godspell* and an exhibition of Marian artwork. We've only sung one crazy song, for a priest friend's ordination anniversary.

At this point, we have about thirty women on the notification list. At any one gathering, we'll get fifteen to twenty, but never the same fifteen to twenty. A few have never attended a meeting, but have asked to stay on the list for prayer and the hope that one day, schedules will align.

When we meet in someone's home, we start with prayer and dinner and small-group chatting and catching up. Then we all gather together and share, usually around a theme that the hostess or Karen and I select. It might be finding Christ in the busyness of work; it might be talking about your confirmation saint or the saint who guides you today. It's also all right to sit quietly. We close by praying for one another's intentions.

In our time together, we've seen some miracles. We've also seen that prayers aren't always answered as quickly as we'd like, or in the form we'd prefer. While we're all of a certain age, we all approach life differently, from unique perspectives and back-grounds. We work at honoring that and at not judging.

As I wrote this book, I thought often of Churchwomen of a Certain Age and how different we are, just as the women I researched were. Initially, I wondered why Elizabeth Canori Mora stayed with her husband or how Maria Goretti, a mere child, found it possible to forgive her murderer. I wondered how Claudine Thévenet, Jeanne Jugan, and others could work with and submit to clergy who tried to kill their charisms. I wondered just how difficult some, like Dorothy Day and Maria Faustina

Kowalska, would have been to be around, given how focused they were on their missions.

Eventually, I realized they were just like my Churchwomen sisters: different, flawed, challenged, difficult—and each one holy in her own way, each one confident in Christ's love and determined to reflect it or share it.

In this book, you'll find a brief reflection that might make you look at Matthew's verses in a new way. You'll also find short essays on how four women saints, blesseds, and servants of God lived each verse, followed by single paragraphs about how four other women did it. You'll find some old friends, such as Bernadette Soubirous, Thérèse of Lisieux, and Frances Cabrini, and some new ones. I pray that you'll see that each of these women was blessed, regardless of the trials she experienced, large or small.

And, I pray that you recognize that blessing in your own busy, complicated existence; that the stories of the women associated with each of the Beatitudes help that blessing come alive for you; and that God brings churchwomen of any age into your life to help celebrate it.

chapter one

SPIRITUAL POVERTY

Blessed are the poor in spirit,
for theirs is the kingdom of heaven.
—MATTHEW 5:3

Interesting, isn't it, that Jesus begins this beautiful sermon by talking about the poor? It was certainly the earthly life he knew: birth in a lowly stable; growing up as a carpenter's son. During his public ministry we learn that he had nowhere to rest his head, that he had no money to render unto Caesar, that those in his hometown thought him to be nothing remarkable. Perhaps that's why he starts the Beatitudes in this way, for he knows the poor are children of the Lord and will see him in heaven.

As followers of Christ, we attempt to recognize him in the least of our brothers and sisters: the poor, the homeless, those discriminated against, the victims, those in prison. They don't always smell good, and they're not always grateful for our love and service. It can be hard to see Jesus in the mentally ill man who spits on us because rather than give him the five dollars he's asked for, we offer to take him around the corner and buy him a meal. But then, maybe it's hard for that man to see Christ in us when we put conditions on assisting him. In blessing the poor, we get a tiny view of the kingdom of heaven in the way we are touched by that interaction.

But Jesus wasn't just talking about physical or economic poverty. He was also talking about spiritual poverty, the only kind many of us in developed countries will ever know firsthand. Jesus knew that kind of poverty too. He showed it to us when he was on the cross. Jesus had let go of everything: his mother, his friends, his public ministry, his garments, his health, his dignity. He asked in that split second why God had forsaken him, and then he turned it over, saying it was finished and giving up the spirit.

We find our own spiritual poverty in many different ways: in humbling ourselves and working and living simply; in stripping ourselves of all the titles and possessions that give us pride; in finding the faith to set aside all the fears and paranoia that give us anxiety. For God to fill us up, we must first empty ourselves of all the stuff that stands between him and us. If we are strong enough to do that—to accept spiritual poverty, to understand that all we need is God and when we have God we have all we need—we begin to see the kingdom of heaven.

And so, we look at the lives of four women who experienced spiritual poverty in very different ways: Chiara Badano, Maria Faustina Kowalska, Jeanne Jugan, and Germaine Cousin.

. . . .
CHIARA BADANO
October 29, 1971—October 7, 1990
Feast Day: October 29

For adults, embracing spiritual poverty is challenging enough. We're afraid of what happens when we put aside our material and emotional "things," good and bad, tangible and intangible, in the name of the kingdom of God. But intellectually, we know the Lord desires to be front and center in our lives, and we trust in his tender mercies when we prostrate ourselves, stripped of everything else, before him. Imagine, however, not being thirty or forty or fifty or older and trying to navigate spiritual poverty with your knowledge and experiences and formation. Imagine being a beautiful, athletic, sixteen-year-old girl, who's just found out she's gravely ill.

Chiara Badano was the apple of her parents' eye. Ruggero and Maria Teresa had been married for eleven years before she was born, and had hoped and prayed to be blessed with a child. And Chiara was a blessing indeed. She was a normal kid, for the most part, like any other child of the era growing up in northern Italy or many other places. She dreamed about being a flight attendant, because the thought of travel was appealing—especially travel to Africa. From an early age, she set aside money for African missions.

Most of the time she was good, so good that in high school some of her classmates taunted her by calling her "Sister," implying she was as holy as a nun. But she wasn't perfect; in fact, she failed a course shortly before her life's turning point, and that failure aggravated her.

Chiara found a special relationship with the Lord early, when she became part of the Focolare Movement, founded in northern Italy in the 1940s. While the founder, Chiara Lubich, was Catholic, the movement also engages with others—Christians, other religions, and even the nonreligious—to promote unity in the world. Through Focolare, Chiara Badano learned about the forsaken Christ on the cross, at that moment of abandonment by his Father. It affected her spirituality deeply, so deeply that her parents agreed to attend a Focolare family gathering the following year. They also found the movement to be a place to grow their faith.

Chiara was on the tennis court when she first felt the pain, so searing that she dropped her racquet. It turned out not to be a muscle tear or strain, but a symptom of bone cancer. One surgery failed, then another. Eventually, she became bedridden. She lost her hair to chemotherapy.

We remember Chiara not for her death, but for the way she ministered to people as she died. When she learned of her diagnosis, she asked for twenty-five minutes by herself. After that, she offered up her suffering to the forsaken Christ, refusing morphine because she wanted to be present to the pain. Before she was bedridden, Chiara would walk about the ward with a chronically depressed young woman, because the walk helped her friend even though it was excruciating for Chiara. There are numerous stories of her friends and caregivers planning to comfort her, only to find themselves comforted instead. For example, she made Valentine's Day dinner reservations for her parents so they would leave the hospital and have some time alone together.

Chiara planned her own funeral—the music, the flowers, the readings—right down to the simple white dress she would be buried in. Her corneas would be donated after her death; the bit of money she had was given to poor children in Africa. She directed that there should be no tears at her funeral, as she would be going to Jesus. Her final words were of consolation to her mother to be happy, because Chiara was. She was beatified in 2010.

While Chiara's dream of traveling to Africa and helping people there did not happen in her lifetime, it has been realized. The Chiara Luce Badano Center in Bénin consists of two family centers, schools, and a chapel for poor or abandoned children.

CHIARA ON SPIRITUAL POVERTY:
"If you want it, Jesus, so do I."[1]

MONSIGNOR LIVIO MARITANO ON CHIARA:
"In the conception of Christianity, Chiara emphasizes what is effectively essential: love for God and his plan of salvation, the centrality of Jesus Christ, obedience to God's will, the supremacy of love in the moral life and the fruitfulness of sacrifice."[2]

REFLECTIONS FOR YOU:
- Share Chiara's story with one of your own children or grandchildren, or, with the parents' permission, a friend's or neighbor's child. Ask the child what makes Chiara special. Listen to the answer.
- Next time you're sick (whether it's a cold or something more serious), model Chiara's example. Be gentle and kind and concerned about the welfare of your caregivers, not just your own aches and pains and fears.
- Consider following Chiara's example and developing some plans for your own funeral, even if it's likely decades away. We don't know when we'll be called. We do know making decisions in times of grief can be difficult for those left behind.

. . . .
MARIA FAUSTINA KOWALSKA
August 25, 1905—October 5, 1938
Feast Day: October 5

It's a moment we sometimes move by quickly in the New Testament, but it's also a moment that is breathtaking: Jesus calls on Peter, Andrew, John, and James to put down their nets and follow him, for he will make them fishers of people. And they do it. No debate, no questions, no protestations about things they have to do before they can follow him. Faustina had a similar moment. It came at a dance.

Faustina, born Helena Kowalska, was the third of ten children. The family was poor, so when she was sixteen, with only three or four years of formal education, Faustina became a housekeeper to help out financially. She had contemplated becoming a nun, but her parents didn't support that dream. Then, one night when she was nineteen, she went to a dance with her sister. While there, Jesus appeared to her and told her to go to Warsaw, eighty-five miles away, and join a convent. Helena bid good-bye to her sister and, without seeing her parents and without knowing a soul in the big city, left on the train. It was the beginning of years of revelations, visions, and prophecies that would lead to development of the Divine Mercy Chaplet. It was also the beginning of years when, apart from Jesus, Mary, and her confessor, Faustina would find herself alone many times.

In Warsaw, she found herself turned down by many convents despite Jesus's direction to her. Imagine the spiritual poverty she must have felt, even fleetingly: after all, she'd held up her part of the bargain! Finally, the Congregation of the Sisters of Our Lady of Mercy agreed to accept Helena—if she saved up enough money to pay for her own habit. It took a year of working as a housekeeper, but she was able to join the congregation and took the name Faustina.

On February 22, 1931, Jesus appeared to her as the King of Divine Mercy, directing her to paint his image with the words "Jesus, I trust in you." He also said that the first Sunday after

Easter should come to be celebrated as the Feast of Mercy. But when Faustina asked her sisters for help with this directive, she received no support. Again, she was alone, except for the Lord.

In May 1933, after she had made her final vows, she was sent to be a gardener to Vilnius, now part of Lithuania. It was there she met Fr. Michael Sopoćko, who, when she initially shared with him her ongoing dialogue with Jesus, ordered a battery of psychiatric tests. Satisfied by the results, he urged her to keep a diary of the messages, and agreed to help her find someone who could fulfill the desire for a Divine Mercy image.

On Good Friday in 1935, Jesus told Faustina he wanted the image, completed the previous year, displayed publicly. This was done on the Sunday after Easter with the local archbishop's permission, with Sopoćko celebrating the Mass.

The following months brought both grace and more distance from Faustina's sisters. The Lord gave her the Divine Mercy Chaplet and its prayers for mercy. About the same time, Faustina felt the need to found a separate congregation of nuns to be devoted to Divine Mercy, and wrote the rules for such a group. Her request was denied, and when she told her superiors she was considering leaving her existing congregation, she found herself sent from Vilnius back to a town near Warsaw, about five hundred miles away.

Never a healthy woman, Faustina's health continued to deteriorate to the point that she was moved to a sanatorium near Krakow. It's now believed that she suffered from tuberculosis. She continued to pray and to record her visions in her diary. Work on materials supporting the Divine Mercy continued and were shared with her. She died on October 5, 1938.

The Divine Mercy devotion served a source of comfort among the Poles during World War II. But then questions arose about the way Faustina had shared it—some thought her writing too self-centered, or not theologically sound—and promotion of it was banned in 1959. However, Karol Wojtyła, then the archbishop of Krakow, began working on her cause for canonization in 1965. Thirteen years later, after the archbishop had become Pope John Paul II, the ban was reversed. In 2000, Faustina was canonized. Today, it is estimated that more than 100 million Catholics worldwide are followers of the Divine Mercy devotion.

FAUSTINA ON SPIRITUAL POVERTY:

"When I was by myself, I began to reflect on the spirit of poverty. I clearly saw that Jesus, although he is Lord of all things, possessed nothing. From a borrowed manger he went through life doing good to all, but himself having no place to lay his head. And on the Cross, I see the summit of his poverty, for he does not even have a garment on himself. ... As exteriorly we should possess nothing and have nothing to dispose of as our own; so interiorly we should desire nothing. And in the Most Blessed Sacrament, how great is your poverty! Has there ever been a soul as abandoned as you were on the Cross, Jesus?"[3]

ST. JOHN PAUL II ON FAUSTINA:

"Her mission continues and is yielding astonishing fruit. It is truly marvelous how her devotion to the merciful Jesus is spreading in our contemporary world and gaining so many human hearts!"[4]

REFLECTIONS FOR YOU:

- Faustina was single-minded in her mission to carry out Jesus's will regarding the Divine Mercy devotion. Clear your life's distractions for thirty minutes today, and invite Jesus to share his will for you.

- Is there some ministry you've put aside because others told you it was silly, wouldn't work, or had been tried before and failed? Pick it up again. Let God, not well-meaning friends and acquaintances, define success for you.
- Incorporate the Divine Mercy Chaplet into your prayer life for the coming week. Journal about where it bears fruit.

· ·

MARY OF THE CROSS (JEANNE JUGAN)
October 25, 1792—August 29, 1879
Feast Day: August 30

Jeanne Jugan was no stranger to the humility associated with spiritual poverty. The founder of the Little Sisters of the Poor came from humble beginnings. Her father died at sea before she was four years old, and her mother struggled to make ends meet for Jeanne and her three siblings and to raise them in the Catholic faith amid the challenges of the French Revolution.

By her mid-teens, Jeanne was working as a kitchen maid, and became inspired by her wealthy employer's generous service to the elderly and the poor. From there, Jeanne became a hospital nurse for six years, and then worked as a servant to an acquaintance she knew through a religious organization. After that employer died, Jeanne, then in her late forties and working as a spinner, took in a disabled elderly woman who was destitute. It is said that Jeanne carried the woman to her dwelling, put her in Jeanne's own bed, then slept in the attic herself. Another woman came, and then another. When Jeanne was fifty, she managed to buy a building that could house forty people. That was the beginning of the Little

Sisters of the Poor, whose rule, written by Jeanne, called for the sisters to beg door to door for what they and the people they served needed. The idea was not only to provide for the elderly poor materially, but to also restore dignity to their lives.

But while Jeanne's accomplishments continued to garner public attention for a time—the French Academy honored her with its Montyon Prize for her humanitarian work—all was not well within her organization. The Rev. Augustin le Pailleur overrode her reelection in 1843 as superior and put in Jeanne's place a twenty-one-year-old nun more malleable to his wishes. He ordered Jeanne into the streets to beg. Jeanne proceeded to do so, humbly and in service to the poor she so loved.

When the sisters' rule was approved and he was named superior general, the priest immediately ordered Jeanne back to the motherhouse and told her to end any contact with benefactors and friends. She spent her final twenty-seven years in retirement, primarily in prayer and contemplation, a true cross for a woman whose life had been devoted to activity and service to those in physical poverty. Her work had been taken from her; her friends and acquaintances had been taken from her. All that remained was the Lord.

Le Pailleur took credit for founding the ministry, and put a plaque on the door to that effect. "You have stolen my work from me, but I willingly give it to you,"[5] Jeanne is said to have told the priest. However, there is no indication she mounted any sort of effort inside or outside the congregation to make their respective roles clear.

When Jeanne died at age eighty-six, many members of her congregation had no idea who she was or what she had done.

Eleven years later, the Holy See investigated le Pailleur and removed him. It took another twelve years, until 1902, before the congregation's true history, crediting Jeanne as the founder, was published. Her path to sainthood began in 1935, and she was canonized in 2009. The sisters continue Jeanne's work today in more than thirty countries on six continents.

JEANNE ON SPIRITUAL POVERTY:
"It is so good to be poor, to have nothing, to depend on God for everything."[6]

A LITTLE SISTERS OF THE POOR SPOKESWOMAN ON JEANNE:
"As much as this (is a) mysterious and painful element in Jeanne Jugan's life for us Little Sisters, we believe that it was part of God's plan, and that without it Jeanne might not have become a saint. We believe that it was her virtue, her heroic humility during many years of trial and injustice, which has made her a saint."[7]

REFLECTIONS FOR YOU:
• Think of a time when a supervisor at work or someone with whom you worked in ministry snatched all the credit and recognition for your accomplishments. Focus your prayers today on forgiving that person, and write him or her a letter to that effect. Mail it if you like.
• Consider volunteering a couple of hours this week at a senior citizens' center or an assisted-living facility, playing games or participating in other activities with the residents. Ask what they are most proud of in their lives. Listen to their stories.
• Is there a special teacher, relative, or other person still alive who had a significant impact on your faith journey? Give that person a call or in-person visit today to say thank you.

• • • • • • • • • • • • • •

GERMAINE COUSIN
1579—1601
Feast Day: June 15

Blended families may be common today with the proliferation of divorce in our country, but common doesn't mean easy. It can be a challenge to open up your heart to the children of your spouse's earlier marriages or relationships and to treat those children with as much love and compassion as you do your own biological children. Consider, then, how much more difficult it was in the sixteenth century—with a stepchild with physical disabilities in a time when people assumed something evil was behind those disabilities. Surely, the child in such a situation would have felt worthless and in despair.

Yet that is the world in which Germaine Cousin lived, suffered, grew—and, with God's love, thrived.

Germaine's right hand or arm was paralyzed at birth, and she suffered from growths on her neck's lymph nodes, which may have been a form of tuberculosis. Her mother died in childbirth or shortly thereafter. It wasn't long after that that her father remarried and began his second family.

Was Germaine's stepmother, Hortense, cruel and evil by nature? Was she jealous of Germaine and insecure about her status as Laurent Cousin's second wife? Was she truly fearful that if her own children spent time with Germaine, they too would develop disabilities? Or was she judgmental in the attitude of the time, that Germaine's birthmother must have done something wrong in God's eyes for the girl to have been born with such limitations? We do know a few things: Hortense gave Germaine leftovers and forced her to crawl on the floor to eat out of the dog's dish. She refused to provide the girl with shoes. She encouraged her children to taunt Germaine and to torture the girl, damaging her clothing, contaminating her food, scalding her with hot water. Ultimately, Hortense ordered Germaine to tend the sheep and sleep in the barn or under a stairwell. Where was Germaine's father during all this? We'll never know.

All Germaine had was her love of God, and it drew her closer and closer to the kingdom of heaven. She was so devoted to daily Mass that when she would hear the bells announcing it was imminent, she would plant her distaff wherever she was and leave the sheep to the tender mercies of her guardian angel. Not a single sheep was ever lost, to wolves or streams or thieves. She managed to fashion a rosary and carried it with her always. She gave to beggars a portion of the small amount of food she received. She helped teach the younger children about faith. Yes, God was all she had, and he was so much that she had to share him.

It is said that a particular incident began to change Hortense's heart and those of the other villagers. The stepmother was about to punish Germaine, believing she had stolen bread and was hiding it in her apron. Germaine opened the apron on that winter day and revealed summer flowers, beautiful and radiant.

Eventually, Germaine was invited back into the house. But she chose to continue life as she had known it. One day, her father went to check on her, concerned she was not up and about and on the way to Mass as usual. At just twenty-two, she had gone on to the kingdom of heaven. But her example of acceptance and embracing spiritual poverty can live on today through each of us.

GERMAINE ON SPIRITUAL POVERTY:
"Dear God, please don't let me be too hungry or too thirsty. Help me to please my mother. And help me to please you."[8]

BLESSED PIUS IX ON GERMAINE:

"Go to Germaine. She is a new star shedding a marvelous glow over the universal Church."[9]

REFLECTIONS FOR YOU:

- Think about the way you interact with your stepchildren or step-grandchildren, or with an acquaintance who has a disability. In what ways does your behavior resemble Hortense's, in thought and attitude, if not in physical punishment? Pray for the grace to overcome this tendency, and the wisdom to understand where it begins.

- Who persecuted you in the past, perhaps through teasing or bullying that the person said was "just joking around"? From the safety of distance, journal about how God helped you through that time and drew you closer to him.

- Consider donating some time, money, or supplies to a shelter for abused children. Perhaps you might want to include some St. Germaine prayer cards as part of that donation.

LEARNING MORE

You may be interested in learning more about these women's examples of spiritual poverty:

- Marta Maria Wiecka, January 12, 1874—May 30, 1904. This Daughter of Charity was a nurse, a good nurse. The hospital patients she tended spoke of her loving service and of her gift as a counselor to those in spiritual crisis or with other problems. Marta endured a false rumor that she had had a relationship with a parish priest's nephew and had become pregnant. Her greatest example of spiritual poverty, of offering up the most valuable thing she had on earth, came when she saw that a male nurse who was a father was frightened about disinfecting the room of a patient with typhoid. She did the work instead, and contracted the disease and died. Marta was beatified in 2008.

- Emilie de Vialar, September 12, 1797—August 24, 1856. Emilie was much like any other wealthy teenage girl in post-revolutionary France. She liked beautiful clothes and jewelry. She ran with the popular crowd, and turned down some marriage proposals. But as time went on, Emilie found herself devoting more time and treasure to the poor in her hometown despite her father's objections. When she was thirty-five, her grandfather, Baron Portal, a former royal physician, died, leaving his considerable estate to Emilie. Rather than spend the money on herself and frivolity, Emilie bought a large building and with three friends began caring for the sick and the poor. Eventually, this ministry became the Congregation of the Sisters of St. Joseph of the Apparition. Emilie was canonized in 1951.

- Kateri Tekakwitha, 1656—April 17, 1680. Kateri didn't have an easy early life. Her Mohawk chieftain father, her mother, and her brother all died of smallpox when she was just four years old, and the disease left the child with poor vision and a badly scarred face. But Kateri was left with one comfort: She remembered her mother, who was Catholic, talking about Jesus. Eventually, Kateri's uncle with whom she lived gave her permission to become a Christian as long as she remained in the village. Still, she suffered persecution and death threats for her religious choice. When Kateri was about twenty-one, she traveled for two months to reach a Catholic mission near Montreal, where she spent the rest of her life. She was canonized in 2012.

- Marie of the Incarnation (Marie Guyart), October 28, 1599—April 30, 1672. This Frenchwoman's story is one of the most difficult of all the saints. Marie's husband died when she was twenty, leaving her with a six-month-old son, Claude. At about the same time, she had a vision of Christ's incarnation and saw herself being saved despite all her flaws. When her son was twelve, Marie left him with relatives and became an Ursuline nun. The parting was wrenching, with Claude attempting to storm the monastery, shouting for his mother's return. About eight years later, Marie led a group of Ursulines headed for what is now Quebec. Claude would go on to become a Benedictine priest and edit his mother's spiritual autobiography; Marie would become known as the mother of the Catholic Church in Canada. She was canonized in 2014.

Summing It Up and Turning It Over

As we grow deeper in spiritual poverty, we grow closer to Christ. From Germaine Cousin, we learn not to obsess about the slights and injustices we experience in our own homes and from family and friends. Jeanne Jugan teaches us to have the grace not to rise to the bait when others, especially those with power over us, angle to take the credit for what we've done, for the Lord knows what happened and that is sufficient. Faustina Kowalska shows us that God desires us to continue down the path he lights, whether or not others think it's where we belong. And in Chiara Badano, we find an example of courage for the time when we prepare to abandon the things and the people we love to join Christ in that final earthly farewell.

Lord, hold my hand. Help me to rely on only you. Help me be brave enough to open my eyes to the kingdom of heaven.

Chapter Two

MOURNING

"Blessed are those who mourn,
for they will be comforted."
—MATTHEW 5:4

How can it be a blessing to mourn? Mourning by its nature means loss and sadness: death of a parent, spouse, child, friend, or someone we know only slightly but considered an inspiration or influence; or, a significant change to one we love, such as a disability or an addiction. There's a diminishment in our lives, and it seems so unfair that the rest of the world keeps on turning as we walk out of the hospital or the funeral home or the halfway house or the rehab center. It just seems wrong that complete strangers are so unaware of our mourning that they still laugh and hold hands, that they still speed and honk their horns.

We also mourn for other losses: our own mobility, due to illness or aging. The end of a treasured romance or friendship. A demotion or change at work. Neighbors who moved. A vacation or season that has come to a close.

Mourning is an integral part of our faith. In his book *The Cross and the Beatitudes: Lessons on Love and Forgiveness*, Fulton J. Sheen put it like this: "We must mourn, first of all, because the world will make us mourn if we follow the Redeemer's beatitudes."[1] We mourn because that is part of the price of following Christ. So much of who and what we are is stripped from us as we strive to put our selfish desires, sins, and temptations aside. It's no easy task to function after either the death of a loved one or the death of a behavior we know in our souls to be displeasing to God.

But in that mourning, we find comfort. When we open up our sorrows and losses, there is also joy in the community that comes together and prepares the funeral liturgy, that arranges for the rides to medical appointments, that makes sure the yard is tended while we are taking part in family therapy half a continent away. When we grieve as community, we also celebrate our ability to love and tend to the broken-hearted.

And always, even if the pain is so minute or so large we cannot or will not share it with our brothers and sisters, we always have the Master Healer, who promises us relief. Jesus, in preparing the disciples for his Passion, compares what will happen to a woman in labor, whose pain is forgotten once the child is born. "So you have pain now; but I will see you again, and your hearts will rejoice, and no one will take your joy from you" (John 16:22).

That faith and confidence that comfort will come if we remain faithful are reflected in the lives of holy women including Anna Schäffer, Claudine Thévenet, Elizabeth Ann Seton, and Louise de Marillac.

．．．．．．．．．．．．．

ANNA SCHÄFFER

February 18, 1882—October 5, 1925

Feast Day: October 5

Mourning can be sharp and deep when we are teenagers: the loss of a first love, perhaps, or the disappointment of not being accepted by the college we want or not getting the summer job for which we know we are perfect. On the cusp of adulthood, we learn anew one of the hardest lessons from childhood: Life isn't always fair.

Perhaps that is also the time that we are first of sufficient intellect to understand that God isn't always fair either, according to our definition of the term, but that he is merciful and has a plan, even though it may not be readily apparent. That is the sort of mourning and acceptance we can learn about from Anna Schäffer, who was canonized in 2012.

Anna's early years were not easy. She was born into a large family in the Bavarian community of Mindelstetten. It was her dream to become a missionary sister. But to become a nun required a dowry, an investment the Schäffers couldn't make. Anna left school and went to work when she was just thirteen to earn money to realize her dream and help support her family.

She was exceedingly troubled by a vision she had when she was sixteen. Later, Anna said the man she saw "held a rosary in his hands, spoke to me of praying the rosary and that (before I was twenty) I would have to suffer a great deal."[2] She was so upset that she refused to return to work and took another job.

Less than three years later, the suffering that had been foretold began. On February 14, 1901, Anna was working as a laundress, and a stovepipe over a boiler became detached. As she attempted to reattach it, Anna, just four days shy of her nineteenth birthday, ended up in a vat of boiling lye, immersing her legs to the knees.

She spent the next fifteen months in the hospital, undergoing a series of unsuccessful operations and suffering almost unbearable pain. Finally, she was released in May 1902, completely bedridden. The situation was exacerbated by the fact that her brother had taken over the family home, and there was no place for Anna there. She and her mother found a room to rent and struggled to live on Anna's disability pension.

Think of the mourning: the loss of a cherished dream of ministry. The loss of mobility by a young, robust woman who had worked hard as a laborer all her teen years. No wonder, then, that reports indicate Anna spent a couple years in what was called "fruitless rebellion" asking the Lord why this had happened to her.

The pain continued, but Anna's acceptance of her situation changed, and with it came comfort, both from Christ and her community. She began doing embroidery work, making church and chapel linens, most often favoring the design of the Sacred Heart to signify Christ's love for his people. She started what would be called her "apostolate of letters," first communicating with others in her village, then with people in Switzerland and Austria, and finally with correspondents as far away as the United States. It became clear that Anna's dream of being a missionary was being realized, just not in the way she had envisioned as a teenager. The pain that bound her to her bed opened her mind to how to comfort others who suffered.

Anna never walked again, and her physical challenges grew. She experienced the stigmata for a time, including reliving Christ's Passion in 1923. Her legs became completely paralyzed; her spinal cord stiffened; she suffered from a form of cancer. Yet her spiritual director at the time said he never heard her complain. Finally, in late August or early September of 1925, she fell out of her bed and suffered a brain injury and could no longer speak. Nonetheless, she communicated via letters until six days before her death.

ANNA ON MOURNING:
"Oh! What happiness and what love are hidden in the cross and suffering!"[3]

BENEDICT XVI ON ANNA:
"She struggled for a time to accept her fate, but then understood her situation as a loving call of the crucified One to follow him."[4]

REFLECTIONS FOR YOU:

- Is there a loss—from yesterday or twenty years ago—that you mourn in a way that interferes with your relationship with God or your community? Consider talking with a priest or spiritual adviser for guidance so that you may find comfort.

- Spend an hour with a friend or acquaintance who suffers from an obvious physical disability—perhaps someone who must use a cane or wheelchair or who uses a service dog. Later, journal about ways you can put what you observed in the way they conduct themselves to work in your life to counter smaller aches and pains.

- Do you have unrealized dreams from childhood, such as Anna's desire to be a missionary? Perhaps it was to be a mother or teacher or a performer. Come up with ways you can stoke that dormant passion to serve God today.

. . . .
CLAUDINE THÉVENET
March 30, 1774—February 3, 1837
Feast Day: February 3

Her name was Claudine, but the family called her Glady. One of seven children, her early years in Lyon, France, passed unremarkably. At the age of nine, she was sent to study at the local

Benedictine abbey, which today is the city's Museum of Fine Arts. When Glady was fifteen, the French Revolution began; she returned home full time, and the nuns were expelled from the abbey three years later in 1792. The old dioceses were no more; now, pastors and bishops would be elected just as civil officials were, and the pope's role would be limited to spiritual guidance in this new world.

Lyon, at the time France's second-largest city, was home to a great deal of conflict between revolutionary groups, and suffered a two-month siege in the summer of 1793. All told, two thousand people were executed in Lyon during the revolution. Two of those executions would affect Glady's life profoundly.

Two of her brothers—Louis-Antoine, who was a year older than she, and François-Marie, a year younger—went missing in the tumult of one of the final battles. Glady searched for them without success, only to arrive home to find they were there. But the reunion was short-lived. Louis-Antoine and François-Marie were turned in by an informant, arrested, and held for execution.

Glady went each day to the execution site in hopes—or dread, perhaps—of seeing her brothers. The fateful day came on January 5, 1794. Before the pair were killed, she had a few seconds with them, taking the letters they had written the family from one brother's shoe. "Forgive, Glady, as we forgive,"[5] he whispered to her. The letters contained similar faith-filled language: "We will be happier than you; in four or five hours, we will be before God. We are going to the bosom of God, this good Father whom we have offended, but we hope completely in His mercy."[6]

Time passed. The revolution ended. Some sort of normalcy resulted, yet people were still dispossessed and suffering. Claudine found a ministry in helping children and young people. When she was about forty, a priest she knew found two children abandoned at a nearby church, and asked for her help. Claudine brought the children to a friend's home. Within a few days, five more were being sheltered. In that same year, 1815, she and some of her friends formed the lay Association of the Sacred Heart, and Claudine was named its president. The association would serve as the foundation for the Congregation of the Religious of Jesus and Mary in 1823, which had as its original goal to provide education and formation for young people up to the age of twenty who were in need. Eventually, the group's ministry expanded to include a boarding school for all social classes.

Amid the success of her ministry, Claudine (known in religious life as Mother Marie Ignatius) experienced more times of mourning. She lived at home until the congregation's founding and when she left, it was difficult for her mother, who died two years later. The priest who had brought those first two children to Claudine's attention died in 1826. Two of the young women in the order on whom she relied greatly also passed away.

In 1836, the year before Claudine's death, another great trial arrived. The order received a new chaplain, François-Xavier Pousset, with the hope that he and Claudine could complete the writing of its constitution. They disagreed on approach, Claudine being more inclined to an approach of Ignatian spirituality, the priest to monastic traditions. After he provided her with last rites less than a week before her death, he accused her of being "an obstacle to the progress of your congregation."[7] Perhaps Claudine thought of her brothers, all those years earlier, and their advice. Her only response was, "How good the Good Lord is!"[8]

The Congregation of the Religious of Jesus and Mary had fallen on hard times at the time of Claudine's death, with just five of the original houses still in operation, all near Lyon. Today, more than a thousand religious provide service in twenty-eight countries.

CLAUDINE ON MOURNING:

"There is no greater tragedy than to live and die without knowing God."[9]

ST. JOHN PAUL II ON CLAUDINE:

"Claudine Thévenet presents herself to us as a model of love and forgiveness."[10]

REFLECTIONS FOR YOU:

- The confidence Claudine's brothers expressed on their way to their execution was breathtaking. Consider time you have spent with people shortly before their death or during a severe illness. Journal about what you have learned from them, and how you have put that wisdom to work to comfort others.

- Sometimes, our actions, while we know they are part of God's plan, can cause others to mourn, as Claudine's decision to leave home did for her mother. Identify a decision that takes you away from people who rely on you. Is there a way you can make the separation a bit easier for them to bear, perhaps through regular phone calls or notes or visits?

- Claudine's ability to keep God foremost in her mind and response as she was challenged by Fr. Pousset shows us how to let parts of us die in service to Christ. What part of you—pride, anxiety, fear—are you being called to let go without mourning?

. . . .

ELIZABETH ANN SETON

August 28, 1774—January 4, 1821

Feast Day: January 4

Sometimes, life is a rollercoaster, full of emotional and material highs only to be followed by the depths of loss, then a swing back up again. As Elizabeth Ann Seton knew, with God as our operating force, the dizzying speed of that rollercoaster needn't disrupt our soul.

The first saint born on U.S. soil was also born into a life of privilege in New York City. Her father, Richard Bayley, was a prominent physician and advocated for public health improvements. Things changed dramatically when Elizabeth was just three. Her mother died, as did a younger sister just eighteen months later. Dr. Bayley remarried within a year; his new wife was not warm to Elizabeth and her older sister, so the girls spent much of their childhood with an uncle about twenty-five miles away in New Rochelle. Elizabeth fell into a period of depression and turned to contemplation of God, journaling, poetry, and music as escapes.

In her late teen years, Elizabeth met William Magee Seton, whose family owned an import-export business. The pair married in 1794, and quickly settled into a lifestyle anyone would have envied: a lovely home in lower Manhattan; a son and a daughter; an active faith life at Trinity Episcopal Church; Elizabeth's charitable ministries, including serving as a founder of the Society for the Relief of Poor Widows with Small Children; all sorts of societal entertainment, including William's cohosting of a ball for President George Washington's sixty-fifth birthday.

However, that earthly happiness would prove to be fleeting. Within five years, the family business began a downward spiral due to political and economic conditions in the United States and Europe, forcing William to file for bankruptcy. To make matters even worse, William learned he suffered from tuberculosis.

By the fall of 1803, the Seton family, which now included five children, was in desperate straits in every way imaginable. It was decided that Elizabeth, William, and eight-year-old Anna Maria would travel to Italy in hopes that the milder climate would ease William's ailments. He had business connections there, including brothers Antonio and Filippo Filicchi.

The Setons arrived to find they would be quarantined for thirty days in a cold, dank military hospital due to a fear of yellow fever. On December 27, less than two weeks after their release, William died, leaving Elizabeth a twenty-nine-year-old impoverished widow with five children, four of them thousands of miles away.

In the United States, Elizabeth's exposure to Catholics had been limited; at that time, the faith was regarded with suspicion by many in the upper class. In Italy, that changed. The Filicchi brothers and their wives took the widow and her daughter under their wing. They showed them Catholic churches and took them to Mass. They listened. They consoled. They provided financial assistance, and one of the brothers even accompanied Elizabeth and Anna Maria back to the United States.

Elizabeth's mind was made up. Despite objections and shunning by friends and family, she converted in 1805. Life in New York became unsustainable, so she accepted an opportunity in 1808 to open a girls' school in Baltimore. The following year, she moved about sixty miles away to a rural area called Emmitsburg, where the Sisters of Charity of St. Joseph, the first original group of women religious in the United States, would be formed.

Life in Emmitsburg was challenging. The women's home wasn't ready when they arrived, so they had to live in a borrowed cabin for six weeks. There were disagreements with two of the Sulpician priests who served as superiors general. The women and their school were often short of funds and space. There was much to mourn, much to question. Yet the sisters persevered and took their first formal vows in July 1813, electing Elizabeth as their mother time and again until her death in 1821. By then, she had buried two of her daughters, two sisters-in-law, and eighteen of her religious sisters at Emmitsburg. In much the same way as she had found comfort in the Lord and Filicchis when William died, so did she find it in her family of sisters.

Elizabeth died of tuberculosis, just as her husband had. But her work lives on today, through the more than five thousand Sisters of Charity who serve in schools, social service centers, and hospitals around the globe.

ELIZABETH ON MOURNING:
"The accidents of life separate us from our dearest friends, but let us not despair. God is like a looking glass in which souls see each other."[11]

CARDINAL TERENCE COOKE ON ELIZABETH:
"In Elizabeth Ann Seton, we have a Saint for our times. In Elizabeth Ann Seton, we have a woman of faith for a time of doubt and uncertainty...a woman of love for a time of coldness and division...a woman of hope for a time of crisis and discouragement."[12]

REFLECTIONS FOR YOU:
• Think of a friend who has lost much in terms of material or emotional support and yet approaches his or her day with faith

and confidence. Ask this person to share the story of the struggle and what faith resources and practices did the most to sustain and comfort him or her.

- The Filicchi brothers and their wives likely didn't think they were doing anything special or extraordinary for Elizabeth and her daughter; they were simply caring for a hurting friend. And yet, their kindnesses had a significant role in her conversion. Identify two acts of kindness you can offer for friends in the coming week without making a big deal out of what you do.

- Remember a time that you felt alone and abandoned by all, including God. If that time has passed, journal about how the experience deepened your faith and your reliance on the Lord. If you are in the midst of the whirlwind, find a way—through a prayer group, retreat, or meeting with a priest or spiritual director—to talk about these feelings. Get some comfort.

. . . .

LOUISE DE MARILLAC
August 12, 1591—March 15, 1660
Feast Day: March 15

Loss and the mourning that accompanies it were Louise's companions from a very early age. Her mother, who was not married to Louise's father, died when Louise was very young. Her father, a member of the French aristocracy, acknowledged his paternity and was initially involved in her life. Then, when Louise was four years old and he married, the child was sent to board at a Dominican convent, where an aunt was among the sisters. When Louise was fifteen, her father died. An uncle was named her guardian, and in the following years, she lived with him at times or in a boarding house. It was during this time that Louise began to think of becoming a Capuchin nun, but was told by the provincial that the Lord had other plans for her.

At twenty-two, Louise married Antoine le Gras, a secretary to the French queen. She busied herself with the Ladies of Charity, an organization of rich women who helped the poor. On Pentecost in 1623, Louise had a vision that she would work with a priest as a woman religious to help the needy. She was concerned about this, given she already had a spiritual director, and wondered whether the vision meant she had erred in marrying. She would later write that she was assured the time would come for these changes, and that put her mind at ease.

Loss and mourning continued to permeate Louise's life. An aunt, godmother to the le Gras's son, died in 1617. Antoine died eight years later. Two uncles with high positions in the government died, one in prison, one in a public execution. In addition, Louise became concerned about her teenage son, who was somewhat spoiled. She fell into a depression.

It was during those dark days that Louise was introduced to Vincent de Paul, a Parisian priest who had established the Confraternities of Charity and who became her spiritual adviser. Vincent was finding that many of the wealthy women attracted to the confraternities had little experience that was beneficial in helping the poor; some lost interest entirely while others sent their servants to do tasks they had agreed to do themselves. Slowly, cautiously, his and Louise's relationship developed, Vincent warning Louise against excessiveness in her spiritual regimen. It was a different sort of comfort than Louise received from her friends, but it was the comfort her mind and soul needed.

Louise began serving as an emissary of sorts for Vincent, conducting site visits and reviewing financial reports of confraternities throughout France. Her aristocratic background and pleasant personality opened doors for the organization; while she had not experienced poverty, her knowledge of loneliness and sorrow helped her establish trusting relationships with those in need.

In November 1633, Louise started training in her home young working-class women for ministries that today we would call social work. Rather than dwelling in a cloistered convent, they lived together in a house, and went among the poor themselves, in peasant dress, to provide service. The women learned to be teachers, give medical assistance, care for orphans, and treat the needy with respect and compassion; they also adopted a regimen for their own spiritual instruction. The women, including Louise, would make formal vows in 1642.

And those wealthy women who hadn't been so suited for direct care? Louise encouraged them to provide financial assistance to the cause, and set up retreats to assist their spiritual growth.

Amid the challenges and victories that came with her work, Louise experienced personal joy. In 1650 her son married Gabrielle Le Clerc and, the following year, Louse's granddaughter Renee-Louise was born.

Vincent and Louise's collaboration lasted for thirty-six years. They both died in 1660, she a few months before him. Today, the Daughters of Charity of St. Vincent de Paul consists of more than seventeen thousand sisters in more than two thousand communities living in ninety-four countries.

LOUISE ON MOURNING:
"God made known to me from my earliest years that it was his will that I should go to him by the way of the Cross."[13]

VINCENTIAN SCHOLAR JEAN MORIN, C.M., ON LOUISE:
"Certainly, much more than Saint Louise, Saint Vincent experienced, for fourteen years, the hardships and injustices of the life of the poor but, much more than Saint Vincent, Saint Louise knew certain sufferings and injustices of life: birth abandonment, illness, death.... Now I understand better all that Saint Louise brought Saint Vincent to help him to organize a more effective service of the poor."[14]

REFLECTIONS FOR YOU:

- Consider the losses you have mourned: the death of a parent, spouse, child, or other loved one, or perhaps a betrayal of trust. How can you use what you learned from that pain to comfort others in your community or elsewhere in the world?
- Think of a friendship or work or ministry relationship that started slowly and cautiously as Louise's and Vincent's did, and has flowered over several years. Handwrite a letter of thanks to the person expressing your gratitude for the ways he or she has helped you grow in faith, confidence, and skill. Give the letter to the person, or if he or she has died, to a member of the family.
- Contemplate Louise's words that it was God's "will that I should go to him by the way of the Cross."[15] How is the Lord drawing you nearer to him by the way of the cross? Discuss this with a priest, spiritual adviser, or trusted friend.

LEARNING MORE
You may be interested in learning more about mourning in the journeys of these women:

- Maria Angela Truszkowska, May 16, 1825—October 10, 1899. Angela was tireless in her work for those who lived in the slums of Warsaw. She was in her thirties when she and a cousin founded what would be known as the Felician Sisters. Angela served as mother superior until her hearing degenerated to the point she no longer felt capable of the role. She was just forty-four. More health issues developed. Rather than mourn the loss of her public ministry, Angela adjusted and spent most of her remaining thirty years praying, sewing, and working in the garden. She was beatified in 1993.

- Paola Elisabetta (Costanza Cerioli), January 28, 1816—December 24, 1865. Sorrow upon sorrow was heaped on Paola Elisabetta's short life. At nineteen, she was forced into marriage with a difficult man forty years her senior. Three of their four children died very young. Then, within the space of a year, her husband and her beloved sixteen-year-old son died. She gave away her wealth and welcomed orphans into her home. Three years later, Costanza founded the Institute of the Sisters of the Holy Family and took the name Paola Elisabetta. She was canonized in 2004.

- Angela Merici, March 21, 1474—January 27, 1540. Angela lost her parents when she was ten and her only sibling not long thereafter. She began establishing schools for girls while she was in her twenties. On a Holy Land pilgrimage when she was fifty, Angela suffered from temporary blindness. Ten years later, she founded the order of the Ursulines to expand her work among young women. Angela was canonized in 1807.

- Hemma of Gurk, c. 980—June 27, 1045. God was the constant in Hemma's life. Her two sons were killed by workers at the mine her nobleman husband owned. His reaction was to seek the deaths of all who had taken part in the related uprising; Hemma convinced him to launch an investigation and to punish only those directly responsible. Later, her husband suffered a violent death as well. Rather than become bitter and renounce the Lord for her tragedies, Hemma founded churches and monasteries and assisted the poor with her wealth. She was canonized in 1938.

SUMMING IT UP AND TURNING IT OVER

Mourning comes in different forms, from the losses of spouses such as Louise and Elizabeth experienced; the deaths of siblings such as Claudine suffered; and the end of dreams we believe will fulfill God's plan for us such as Anna endured. It's hard when we are doing the best at what we believe is our call, only to have it snatched away. These women's stories show us that if we trust in God and our community in our mourning, we will learn how to provide succor to others who mourn, and emerge all the closer to the Lord on the other side.

Lord, in good times and bad, draw me closer to you. Let me trust in you to turn my mourning into joy and gladness.

Chapter Three

MEEKNESS

"Blessed are the meek,
for they will inherit the earth."
—MATTHEW 5:5

The words *meek* or *meekness* appear just nine times in the *New Revised Standard Version* of the Bible, five times in the Old Testament, and four times in the New.

Psalm 10 calls on the Lord to hear "the desire of the meek"; Psalm 37 foretells that the meek "shall inherit the land," perhaps one of the verses Jesus had in mind when he taught the crowd. Sirach 45 speaks of Moses's selection by the Lord for his "faithfulness and meekness." Isaiah 11 and 29 also promise a better world for the meek. In 2 Corinthians, Paul defends his ministry "by the meekness and gentleness of Christ"; Colossians advises that we clothe ourselves "with compassion, kindness, humility, meekness, and patience." James 1:21 urges us to cast off our wickedness "and welcome with meekness the implanted word that has the power to save your souls." The following verse in James 1 is perhaps even more telling as to the author's view of what meekness means: "But be doers of the word, and not merely hearers who deceive themselves."

In today's world, *meek* gets a bad rap. We link it to words like *submissive* and *deferential*, words that might make for a deeper relationship with God in theory but that make us uncomfortable to say, let alone consider using as guideposts in our relationships with others here on earth. We want to be strong, empowered, confident, successful, popular—not meek, for goodness' sake!

The thing is, we become all of those things when we embrace meekness and humility. It is through those attributes that we prepare ourselves to "inherit the earth." In his sermon on the Beatitudes back in the fifth century, St. Leo the Great explained the last part of the verse in this way:

> The earth, then, which is promised to the meek, and is to be given to the gentle in possession, is the flesh of the saints, which in reward for their humility will be changed in a happy resurrection, and clothed with the glory of immortality, in nothing now to act contrary to the spirit, and to be in complete unity and agreement with the will of the soul.[1]

Strength, not weakness, surely is what Jesus had in mind when he threw down the challenge of this Beatitude. It takes a lot of strength and faith to offer ourselves, our gifts and our weaknesses, our very lives, for God and his people. It takes more than talk; it takes a willingness to acknowledge God as all knowing and all powerful, and the courage to humble ourselves in our encounters with the body of Christ. Jesus knew this himself. Consider his agony in the garden, when he asked if the cup might pass him, or the wedding at Cana, when his Spirit-filled mother had to nudge him into beginning his public ministry, or his initial reluctance to help the Canaanite woman whose daughter was tormented by a demon. It's human to feel challenged by the sort of meekness God desires, but with his help, we can be courageous enough to be obedient and faithful enough to believe in our inheritance to come in the next world.

That willingness and courage is reflected in holy women including Gianna Beretta Molla, Paulina do Coração Agonizante de Jesus, Thérèse of Lisieux, and Bernadette Soubirous.

· · · · · · · · · · · · · · · · · ·
GIANNA BERETTA MOLLA
October 4, 1922—April 28, 1962
Feast Day: April 28

Gianna Beretta Molla was one of those women who appeared to have it all, one of those women for whom everything seems to come effortlessly.

Gianna, an attractive brunette with a winning smile, was in the midst of an impressive career as a pediatrician. She and her loving husband of six years had three beautiful children under the age of five. And then there were her ministries, including much time spent with Catholic Action and the Society of St. Vincent de Paul in her early years. She was an avid skier and mountain climber, and enjoyed the fine arts—concerts, the theater, and the opera. It was a busy life, a very happy life, and Gianna wasn't even forty yet. There had been some sadness—her pregnancies had all been challenging, with long, difficult deliveries, and she had suffered two miscarriages—but everyone was all right now, and another baby was on the way.

Then, in September 1961, two months pregnant, Gianna learned she had a large fibroid growth in her uterus. She rejected the first two treatment options: complete hysterectomy with the loss of the baby, or removal of the growth and termination of the pregnancy.

Rather, she opted for the third option, which was to remove the fibroid and continue the pregnancy. The instructions Gianna gave her medical team were that if a choice had to be made, to save the baby. That's not to say her death would be a certainty; indeed, Gianna's husband, Pietro, said while she was in the hospital, she leafed through fashion magazines looking at clothes she wanted to buy when she returned home.

However, that was not meant to be. Gianna Emanuela Molla was born April 21; Gianna herself died a week later of an infection that fifty years later almost certainly would not have been fatal. Gianna Emanuela would grow up to become a doctor, and care for her father in the years before his death at age ninety-seven.

It's one thing to say what we would be willing to sacrifice for God or our family or the body of Christ when we're talking in theory. It's quite another to proceed with a decision knowing, as Gianna did given her professional training, the earthly risks with obeying God's will. Some of the saint's writing seems prescient, including this: "Look at the mothers who truly love their children: how many sacrifices they make for them. They are ready for everything, even to give their own blood so that their babies grow up good, healthy, and strong."[2]

While Gianna's meekness at that crucial point is inspirational, it was not the only time she humbled herself in a challenging situation, praying for guidance and reaching out to trusted family and friends and accepting God's will.

When she was young, low grades sometimes kept her from advancing in classes, and once caused her to miss a family vacation. Before Gianna was twenty, she lost both her parents in a four-month period. She had a strong desire to join her brother, a

Capuchin priest and missionary, in Brazil after she had finished her studies and gone into practice. The process to make that happen dragged on for a variety of reasons, and she went to Lourdes on a pilgrimage to discern God's will for her. The result? She saw her vocation would be to have a family, and abandoned her dream of becoming a missionary.

The strength of Gianna's faith and her willingness to submit are shown in the way she lived her life and in her writings, including this: "Everything has a particular end and obeys a law. Everything develops toward a predestined end. God has traced a way for each one of us, our vocation and a life of grace together with our physical life.... Both our earthly and eternal happiness depends on following our vocation very carefully."[3]

GIANNA ON MEEKNESS:
"O Jesus, I promise you to submit myself to all that you permit to happen to me. Only make me know your will."[4]

ST. JOHN PAUL II ON GIANNA:
"This holy mother of a family remained heroically faithful to the commitment she made on the day of her marriage. The extreme sacrifice she sealed with her life testifies that only those who have the courage to give of themselves totally to God and to others are able to fulfill themselves."[5]

REFLECTIONS FOR YOU:
- Reread Gianna's words about mothers and their children. Consider how her words reflect God the Father's love for all of us, and Jesus's sacrifice for us.
- Think of a time that you made an easy choice, and it turned out to have far more profound results than you expected. Perhaps

it was to go on a date with a friend's brother you ended up marrying or to take an internship because it was close to your home, only to go on to work for the establishment for a decade or more. Journal about the way God was guiding your path without you being conscious of it, and when you first realized he was involved in the process.

• Offer up a novena or other quiet prayer time for a friend who is in what seems to be a no-win dilemma. Then set aside some time to listen to him or her, and provide guidance if appropriate.

. . . .

Paulina do Coração Agonizante de Jesus
December 16, 1865—July 9, 1942
Feast Day: July 9

Brazil's first female saint, born Amabile Lucia Visintainer, learned early about taking risks and making bold moves, skills that seem contrary to meekness.

Amabile, who was of Germanic ancestry, was born in what is now Italy but at the time was part of the Austro-Hungarian empire. The family had little money, and Amabile took at job at the local silk mill when she was just eight. Shortly before her tenth birthday in 1875, her family became part of a wave of Europeans who immigrated to Brazil. Imagine the change in language, geography, and customs! The girl received little formal education, but helped out with catechism and cleaning tasks at her parish. She was busy at home as well; her mother died when Amabile was twenty, and she had to care for her dozen brothers and sisters and run the household as her father worked out of town during the week.

When she was twenty-four, Amabile and a friend began caring for a woman who was dying of cancer. A third woman soon joined their community, which became the Congregation of the Little Sisters of the Immaculate Conception, with the women taking their vows in 1895. It was the first order of women religious founded in Brazil. It was at this time that Amabile took the religious name Paulina do Coração Agonizante de Jesus, or Paulina of the Agonizing Heart of Jesus.

In 1903, the congregation elected Paulina as superior general for life. More bold actions followed. She moved from southern Brazil's farming area to bustling São Paulo, more than two thousand miles away. It was a time of change: Brazil had become a republic in 1889, and the year before slavery had been abolished. The convent Paulina opened in the city focused on caring for elderly former slaves, orphans, and the children of former slaves. Five more Little Sisters of the Immaculate Conception convents were established.

And then, in 1909, her life took a drastic turn. The congregation was experiencing turmoil, later described by a distant relative as "injustice and false accusations."[6] São Paulo's first archbishop, Duarte Leopoldo e Silva, believed the best way to resolve the situation was to remove Paulina from all leadership positions, saying she "should live and die as an underling."[7] The archbishop's recollection was that Paulina willingly accepted the demotion. There would be no more trailblazing, no more large-scale relocations or projects of the sort that had marked Paulina's life to this point. There is no evidence she fought to regain power; instead, she spent the next nine years as a hospice and hospital worker fifty miles away, praying for the community she had helped found.

Finally, in 1918, the archbishop and superior general allowed her to return to the mother house. It was a quiet life, spent praying and helping ailing sisters, save for her acknowledgment as Venerable Mother Foundress when the Holy See recognized the order with a decree of praise in 1933.

Paulina's final years were fraught with health issues. She suffered from diabetes, which led to complications when she injured a finger. The finger eventually was amputated; later, she lost her entire right arm. In her final months, she was totally blind. Still, Paulina never appeared to question whether God had abandoned her, telling her spiritual director shortly before her death: "The presence of God is so intimate to me that it seems impossible for me to lose it; and such presence gives my soul a joy which I cannot describe."[8]

ARCHBISHOP DUARTE LEOPOLDO E SILVA ON PAULINA:
(When Paulina was informed she was being removed as superior general,) "She threw herself on her knees...she humbled herself...she answered that she was most ready to hand over the congregation.... She offered herself spontaneously to serve the congregation as an underling."[9]

PAULINA ON MEEKNESS:
"Be humble. Trust always and a great deal in divine providence; never never must you let yourselves be discouraged, despite contrary winds. I say it again: trust in God and Mary Immaculate; be faithful and forge ahead!"[10]

REFLECTIONS FOR YOU:
• Think of a time when you suffered a disappointment or public humiliation. What healing balm did a family member, friend, or perhaps complete stranger offer? What lesson in meekness did you learn? Even if it's been years since the incident, write the person a note of thanks, even if you don't send it.

- Is there a ministry or professional situation in which you have remained out of ego's sake or complacency, even though you are no longer the best person for the position? Ask a trusted party to help you plan a transition strategy.
- Submitting to God sometimes means taking on a role we're not sure we're ready for, as Paulina may have done in caring for her brothers and sisters. Pray for the courage to trust God's direction when his desire for you is made clear.

• • • • • • • • • • • • • • • •

Thérèse of Lisieux
January 2, 1873—September 30, 1897
Feast Day: October 1

Her sister ordered her to write the book. It wasn't something Thérèse burned to do. She told another woman religious who wanted to write her memoirs, "The great graces of one's life, such as one's vocation, can't be forgotten. The memory of those graces will avail you more if you confine yourself to going over them in your mind, than if you write them down."[11] But Thérèse's sister and Carmelite prioress, Agnes of Jesus, asked her to compile her childhood memories, and so she did, showing the humility and obedience that typifies spiritual meekness. The writing of the first part of *The Story of a Soul* took about a year, was finished on the Feast of St. Agnes, and was dedicated to her sister.

"The day you asked me to do it, I thought it might be a distraction to me," Thérèse confesses on the opening page of the work, "but afterwards, Jesus made me realize that simple obedience would please him best."[12]

The Little Way was not always an easy one for Thérèse. Her mother died before Thérèse was five. She was a bit of a high-strung child who craved the limelight. A change began shortly before her fourteenth birthday when she overheard her father complain about the need to put Christmas presents in the shoes of someone that age. While Thérèse at first was hurt by the comment, she swallowed her initial reaction without sharing it with her father and did her best to keep the event's tone as light and happy as ever. Thérèse put her family before her own hypersensitivity with this meekness. It was a pattern she would attempt to follow the rest of her life.

In the next year or so, she would exhibit a memorable example of faithful strength through meekness. She burned to join three of her sisters in the religious life despite her youth. First, a priest told Thérèse she would need to wait until she was twenty-one. Then, a bishop told her he needed to think about her request. While his decision was still pending, Thérèse was part of a pilgrimage to Rome. She took advantage of an audience with Pope Leo XIII in November 1887 to plead her cause directly. A little more than a month later, the bishop granted her immediate entry, but the mother superior advised Thérèse she would need to wait until April. As disappointed as Thérèse was not to enter the Carmel right away, she accepted the decision. It was a sign of her growing trust in God and his will for her.

Later, Thérèse accepted with the same grace a decision that she would remain an unprofessed novice eight months longer than the standard year. She would remain a professed novice the rest of her short life, staying in the novitiate rather than making her solemn profession. She bore much from her fellow women religious: an older nun who complained Thérèse was too young and too impatient to help her. A nun who seemed to delight in splashing her face with dirty laundry water. A superior who called her a "spoilt middle class"[13] girl. The once self-absorbed Thérèse learned to hold back her responses…and to serve with humility. She exhibited that same humility in accepting the suffering tuberculosis brought her in the closing years of her life.

And in her meekness, the child who said from a very early age she wanted to be a saint left behind her impatience, her egotism, and her strong will to become a doctor of the Church for her writings on prayer.

THÉRÈSE ON MEEKNESS:
"…Dear Lord, Thou knowest my weakness. Each morning I resolve to be humble, and in the evening I recognize that I have often been guilty of pride. The sight of these faults tempts me to discouragement; yet I know that discouragement is itself but a form of pride. I wish, therefore, O my God, to build all my trust upon Thee. As Thou canst do all things, deign to implant in my soul this virtue which I desire, and to obtain it from Thy Infinite Mercy, I will often say to Thee: 'Jesus, Meek and Humble of Heart, make my heart like unto Thine.'"[14]

CARDINAL FRANCIS BOURNE ON THÉRÈSE:
"I love St. Thérèse of Lisieux very much because she has simplified things: in our relationship with God she has done away with the mathematics."[15]

REFLECTIONS FOR YOU:
• We all know people who second-guess our decisions, who "just want to help" by attempting to fix our problems, who don't listen to us when we talk. How can you use Thérèse's example to reform this relationship or your role in it?
• Are you too fearful or too proud to submit to what you know in your soul is what God desires of you in a situation? Consider

discussing your inner conflict with someone you trust. Pray for strength.

- Sometimes, it's time to relinquish our seat at the bridal table. What ministry or professional role are you clinging to because you have allowed it to define you? Journal about how you might pass the torch to someone else. The person may not do the work the way you do it, but what needs to get done will get done. Set a timetable. Then follow it.

. . . .

BERNADETTE SOUBIROUS
January 7, 1844—April 16, 1879
Feast Day: April 16

Most of those who lived in the French village of Lourdes probably hadn't given Bernadette Soubirous more than a passing thought. She lived with her parents, sister, and two brothers in a one-room cottage that held just three beds and at one time had served as a jail cell. Bernadette, the oldest child, was functionally illiterate in part because her illnesses—asthma, and a bout with cholera when she was six—made regular school attendance problematic. She wasn't a child who drew much attention to herself, and at fourteen, had yet to make her First Communion.

Yet it was to this simple, sickly young woman that the Blessed Virgin chose to make an appearance on February 11, 1858, as Bernadette struggled to join up with her sister and a friend while they collected firewood near a river bank. She turned to see a beautiful lady in a white dress with a belt, and two yellow roses at her feet. Bernadette and the lady joined in a rosary, and when they were finished, the lady vanished. Bernadette saw her again the following Sunday. When she visited a third time, the lady asked

Bernadette to come every day for fifteen days and to see that a chapel was built on the site.

Bernadette saw the lady eighteen times in the next six months (and made her First Communion). The lady identified herself as the Immaculate Conception, the term pronounced *ex cathedra* by Pope Pius IX just four years earlier to describe Mary's conception without original sin. It was a term with which Bernadette had no familiarity. The girl's acceptance of what she was told, and her honesty and spiritual indifference to questioning by civil and clerical authorities exhibited strength in meekness. Her witness never wavered. Bernadette had seen what she had seen, and had heard what she had heard. Whether people believed her was of little account to her. What mattered was the lady's message of penance and prayer, including the request for a chapel at the site. When challenged about the visions, Bernadette would simply say the lady asked her to tell people what she saw, not to make them believe her.

And, indeed, initially, people did question Bernadette's veracity and sanity, in particular when the Blessed Virgin told her to drink and wash in the spring. There was no spring to be seen. Nonetheless, Bernadette dug her hands into the earth, covering her face in mud as a tiny trickle of water was released. Within a few hours, the trickle swelled to a stream; within a month, two people said they had been healed by the waters. Millions have visited Lourdes since in gratitude for or in search of cures, and the Church has recognized dozens of miraculous healings there.

And what of Bernadette? She continued to be besieged by both skeptics and believers, and eventually joined a convent, not even leaving to attend the opening of the Lourdes basilica in 1876.

While some remarked on the glow on her face when she was at prayer or in conversation with them, her superior general said, "She is good for nothing."[16] From all appearances, Bernadette was as unconcerned about slights such as this as she had been by those who called her a fool as a child. Perhaps she thought of what the Blessed Virgin had told her: "I do not promise to make you happy in this life, but in the other."[17]

Bernadette suffered from tuberculosis and died when she was just thirty-five. She was canonized in 1933 for her general obedience, faithfulness, and prayer life, not specifically because of her encounters with the Blessed Virgin.

BERNADETTE ON MEEKNESS:
"The Blessed Virgin chose me only because I was the most ignorant."[18]

BENEDICT XVI ON BERNADETTE:
"The day of St. Bernadette's feast is also my birthday. This fact already makes me feel very close to this little saint, this little girl, young, pure, and humble, with whom our Virgin speak. To encounter this reality, this presence of the Blessed Virgin in our times, to see the traces of this young girl who was a friend of the virgin and moreover, to meet the virgin, her mother, is a very important event for me."[19]

REFLECTIONS FOR YOU:
• Where is one of your strongest beliefs being challenged by a family member or friend? Perhaps it's your view on abortion or immigration reform. Pray with Bernadette to find the words to state your position clearly, calmly, and non-defensively.
• John the Baptist said he was unworthy to unfasten Jesus's sandal, yet Jesus serenely instructed his relative to baptize him.

What is Christ calling you to do that you feel totally unqualified to do? How can Bernadette's example help you put those feelings aside?

• Spend some one-on-one time with the Blessed Virgin. Listen to what she has to share. What is it she desires you do to honor her Son in this world?

LEARNING MORE

You may be interested in learning more about meekness in the journeys of these women:

• Rafqa Pietra Choboq Ar-Rayès de Himlaya, June 29, 1832—March 23, 1914. In 1885, more than thirty years after this Lebanese woman took her religious vows, she asked to feel some of Jesus's Passion. Headaches started immediately, and she had no real relief until her death. She eventually lost her sight and was paralyzed, but still praised God. Rafqa was canonized in 2001.

• Catherine Labouré, May 2, 1806—December 31, 1876. The Blessed Virgin asked this twentysomething woman religious to create a medal, the one we know today as the Miraculous Medal (depicting Mary standing on a globe, foot crushing a serpent's head, light streaming from her hands). The Blessed Virgin's request accomplished, Catherine went to work caring for aged men and didn't speak again of the special assignment she had fulfilled until just before her death, nearly fifty years later. Catherine was canonized in 1947.

• Anna Maria Taigi, May 29, 1769—June 9, 1837. This Roman housewife and Trinitarian tertiary began having visions when she was barely in her twenties. One of the preeminent mystics of her day, Anna Maria was obedient to God's use of her as a healer and to his desires to speak with her, even during meals with her family. She was beatified in 1920.

- Humility, c. 1226—May 22, 1310. Humility was from a wealthy Italian family. She joined a monastery when her husband did, and became a recluse while she was still in her twenties. Perhaps her greatest obedience came twelve years later, when she agreed to leave her cell and found a new monastery, where her writing flowered. Humility was canonized in 1720.

Summing It Up and Turning It Over

Meekness can mean holding back our very human reactions to slights from other people, as Thérèse and Bernadette show us. It can also mean being accepting of the type of attacks and humiliation Paulina experienced, and being so trusting of God's plan for us that we turn over our very lives to him, as Gianna did. It's no wonder Jesus praised the meek, for spiritual meekness at its core is all about strength and faith.

Lord, please fill my heart and soul with the confidence that you will always provide what I need, when I need it, and let me be obedient to you.

Chapter Four

RIGHTEOUSNESS

"Blessed are those who hunger and thirst for righteousness,
for they will be filled."
—MATTHEW 5:6

There's nothing quite as annoying as a self-righteous Christian. You know, the one who's sure the way he or she lives his or her life is better than the way you or anyone else live yours. The person is quite vocal about his or her virtues and good works, and quite eager to judge yours and let you know where you're just not giving enough or doing enough, or where you're not giving or doing the right things. Does that sort of attitude do anything to encourage self-examination or change? Of course not! Either we ignore or avoid the person, or judge him or her in turn. Self-righteousness can breed self-defensiveness.

Take out the "self" (why is it that faith so often calls us to do that?) and you've got an entirely different dynamic. What is righteousness? As Catholics, we're told in the *Catechism* that it starts with the Lord: "Justification is at the same time *the acceptance of God's righteousness* (emphasis original) through faith in Jesus Christ. Righteousness (or 'just') here means the rectitude of divine love. With justification, faith, hope, and charity are poured into our hearts, and obedience to the divine will is granted us" (CCC 1991).

The word *rectitude* communicates a moral integrity, a straight-ness and a rightness, if you will. But it's not a self-righteousness; we know we are flawed, and our path to salvation is through faith and the cleansing of our souls by the Holy Spirit through baptism. Once on that path, we can't stay quiet about the gifts we have received. It's not that we're better or smarter or holier than anyone else. It's about desiring to share the Good News with others inside and outside our faith, with those who hunger and thirst for it, knowingly or unknowingly.

The Gospel of John tells us that among the final words of Jesus were: "I am thirsty" (19:28). Did he really want that sponge of wine that was offered up? Probably not. He had told his followers earlier that those who believed would never hunger or thirst. Jesus thirsts for us, because when we are one with him, we too are sati-ated. In turn, we can help sate the hunger and thirst of others by bringing them to him, flawed as we are, flawed as they are. We do this by living authentic, spirit-filled lives that reflect our journey toward righteousness, and by inviting others to do the same regardless of whether they're family members, longtime adversaries, or complete strangers.

The search to feed ourselves and others in Christ isn't always easy. We will be laughed at, ignored, threatened, and worse. But the option of staying quiet and going hungry is closed to us by our baptism. Dining with and in the Master is the only way.

Let's consider the ways in which four women—Laura Montoya y Upegui, Hildegard Burjan, Mariam Thresia Chiramel Mankidiyan, and Teresa of Avila—journeyed to righteous fulfillment.

························
LAURA MONTOYA Y UPEGUI
May 26, 1874—October 21, 1949
Feast Day: October 21

The first thing you notice when you see images of Laura Montoya y Upegui isn't her face or her veil. Your eyes are drawn to the emblem on her habit's chest. It says *Sitio*, Latin for "I thirst," those words Christ said on the cross, and her congregation's motto. And thirst—for Christ and for the souls she desired to bring him, souls so many thought were worthless—is exactly what Laura burned to do.

From an early age, Laura knew what it was like to have people discount your abilities based on your socioeconomic status. The second of three children, her family was torn apart by her father's death in the Colombian civil war when she was just two. Laura was sent to be raised by her grandmother, but was only able to go to school for a year as there was no money for books. When the girl was sixteen, her mother said she needed to help the family financially. Laura was able to enter a teachers' school, where she excelled at her studies and dreamed of becoming a cloistered Carmelite. It was perhaps understandable, given her love for the Lord and the upheaval she had seen in her short life. Sometimes, we thirst for quiet contemplation.

In 1908, Laura went to a remote area to serve as a teacher, and also became a missionary of sorts, educating the indigenous people about Christ, and in some cases introducing him to them. Her heart and soul warmed to the work, especially when she saw mistreatment of those she was growing to love. The experience made her reconsider her desire to be part of a cloister. Instead, she founded the Missionaries of Mary Immaculate and St. Catherine of Siena community.

Just before her fortieth birthday, she and four other women left the city of Medellín to minister to those in what at the time was a more remote area about a hundred miles away. The women came under criticism, for such missions in Latin America were rarely successful and typically were headed by men when they were attempted. Some questioned the effort by the calling the people the women were going to aid "wild beasts."[1] But Laura didn't care; she believed in her heart and soul and based on her earlier experience that these Colombians hungered and thirsted to know Jesus whether or not they were aware of it. It was simply her job and that of her congregation to provide an introduction.

In the jungle, the women rode mules and lived simply, in huts without walls and dressing as much like the indigenous people as possible. Their approach was to engage the Colombians as they were, rather than attempt to change their lifestyle. They were forced to leave one area of the country in 1925, but were welcomed elsewhere.

Laura continued to advocate for those living on Colombia's margins, even as she spent the final nine years of her life in a wheelchair. Canonized in May 2013, she continues to serve as a strong role model for South America's young women who hunger and thirst for righteousness, regardless of their socioeconomic status.

LAURA ON RIGHTEOUSNESS:
"Lord, destroy me and, upon my ruins, build a monument to your glory."[2]

POPE FRANCIS ON LAURA:
"[She] teaches us to see the face of Jesus reflected in the other, to overcome indifference and individualism, welcoming everyone

without prejudice or constraints, with love, giving the best of ourselves and above all, sharing with them the most valuable thing we have...Christ and his Gospel."[3]

REFLECTIONS FOR YOU:

- In whom do you find it difficult to see Christ's face: those of another gender, another ethnicity, another age? Consider looking for safe but challenging opportunities to spend time with someone whose outward appearance makes you feel uncomfortable.

- As you go about your day, make a list of the stereotypical thoughts that come into your mind, even if you don't verbalize them: people of a particular ethnicity are hard workers or lazy, people who live in a particular neighborhood are snobs or criminals, people who dress in a particular way are tramps or drug dealers. At the end of the day, pray for the Lord's help in banishing those notions from your mind and soul and to accept people as they are, as Christ does.

- How do you present yourself when you help out at a food pantry or homeless shelter or home for abused women? Do you deck yourself all out in jewelry and makeup and expensive clothes, or do you attempt to dress more like the people you serve? How would Jesus dress when doing this ministry?

· · · · · · · · · · · · · · ·

HILDEGARD BURJAN
January 30, 1883—June 11, 1933
Feast Day: June 12

Hildegard's journey from second daughter of non-practicing Jewish parents to one of the first women in the Austrian Parliament to beatification in 2012 is a story of hunger and thirst—and fulfillment in Christ.

Born in Germany, Hildegard Freund attended the University of Zurich, studying philosophy, literature, and sociology, and attaining a doctorate at a time when that was a relative rarity for women. Two of her professors there focused on Jesus's teachings on social justice and human dignity, which spoke profoundly to Hildegard. She thought then about converting to Catholicism, but still had doubts. While in school, she met Alexander Burjan, and they married in May 1907 and moved to Berlin.

In October 1908, Hildegard was taken to the hospital with acute abdominal pain, which was diagnosed as renal colic, most commonly associated with kidney stones. Four major surgeries provided no relief, and the doctors were close to giving up on her case. Then, on Easter Sunday, April 11, the pain abated at last. Hildegard was especially struck by the faith and care she had been provided by the hospital's nursing staff, the Sisters of Mercy of St. Borromeo. She was baptized four months later, followed by Alexander's baptism a year later.

The Burjans then moved to Austria. It was not long, however, before the young couple faced another crisis: Hildegard was pregnant, and because of her health history, physicians recommended she abort the baby. She adamantly refused, and on August 27, 1910, their only child, Lisa, was born. Mother and daughter were both healthy.

As Alexander's career progressed, the couple became more and more involved in Viennese society, which Hildegard parlayed into gaining support for the social justice passions that had had their first stirrings back in Zurich. She was especially interested in advancing equal rights and human dignity for working women and mothers. In 1912, she founded the Association of Christian

Outworkers, which led to more support for maternity leave and other assistance for new mothers as well as job training for young women. Through that work, Hildegard also drew attention to the need for reform of child labor laws. She became a strong advocate for equal pay for equal work for women, and in November 1918, was in charge of the first formal political gathering of Christian women. The assembly came just a month after Austrian women gained the right to vote and run for office.

Hildegard's activities and charism did not go unnoticed. The Christian Socialist Party asked her to run for the National Assembly. While she was reluctant to do so, given her health and obligations at home, she ultimately said yes because she saw it as a duty to Christ to use any influence she had to help those living on society's margins. She won election, the only female Christian Socialist Party delegate, and one of only a handful of women in the assembly.

Hildegard served only two years, but advanced an aggressive agenda: equality of the genders in the workplace and public life; more money for education of girls and women; more support for expectant and new mothers. One of her greatest accomplishments was a law that set minimum wages and working conditions for household workers.

Hildegard chose not to seek reelection in 1920, in part due to her health, in part due to simmering tension over her Jewish ethnicity, but also because she had found a new way to slake her spiritual thirst and that of others. On October 4, 1919, Hildegard had founded the Sisters of Caritas Socialis (Sisters of Social Charity), a group of women religious and lay associates devoted to helping the underprivileged and those despised by society, such as prostitutes, the homeless, and unwed mothers.

In 1938, many of the organizations Hildegard had been involved with were banned when Germany annexed Austria. After World War II, Caritas Socialis was reestablished and remains today an organization committed to social service.

Hildegard on Righteousness:

"The more someone is convinced of and steeped in his conviction, the more he will calmly tolerate different opinions, the more he will seek what reconciles and unites; the more he will ignore what divides in working together."[4]

Cardinal Christoph Schönborn on Hildegard:

"She committed herself with an open heart for the adversities in her time to fight for the rights of the underprivileged and against social exclusion of disadvantaged groups by society."[5]

Reflections for You:

- Cradle, convert, or revert: Have you had an "aha" moment when you said to yourself, "That's why I'm Catholic"? Talk with members of your prayer group about similar moments each of you has felt.
- Hildegard was passionate about seeing that women got a fair chance in life. Is there something you can do—donate some time or gently used "interview ready" clothing at a women's shelter, perhaps—to help your sisters who are a little down on their luck?
- Politics isn't a spectator sport. Write an e-mail or letter or sign a petition to a local official or government agency expressing your view on a controversial issue.

. . . .

MARIAM THRESIA CHIRAMEL MANKIDIYAN
April 26, 1876—June 8, 1926
Feast Day: June 8

Spiritual thirst and hunger—not to mention confusion—were the hallmark of the first half or so of Blessed Mariam Thresia's life. That she persevered and went on to be what some call the Teresa of Calcutta of her day is an example of how faith challenges can ultimately bring us closer to Christ and our brothers and sisters.

Thresia was born in far southwestern India in what is now the state of Kerala during the time of British rule. She was born the third of five children into a family that had had influence in the past, but had fallen on hard times due to her father's need to finance numerous dowries, including seven for his sisters and two for his daughters. Both Thresia's father and a brother used alcohol to deal with the pressures; her mother, who had been an important spiritual influence on Thresia, teaching her to make the Sign of the Cross before she was four, died when her daughter was twelve. The time also marked the end of Thresia's formal education.

In 1902, a parish priest, Fr. Joseph Vithayathil, agreed to serve as Thresia's spiritual director. It was a relationship that would last the rest of her life, and one that would be critical in the next seven years when her thirst for righteousness would be tested severely.

Thresia had tried to enter several convents but failed, due to her family's social standing or the lack of a sufficient dowry. She also considered living as a hermit, and that didn't work either. And while she was blessed with numerous encounters with the Holy Family and the Blessed Mother, levitations, and ecstasies during this time, she was also beset by demons with such severity that the bishop approved exorcisms for her. Starting in January 1902, Thresia on a regular basis was stoned, beaten, and tempted by the evil spirits, primarily during the night. Finally, in December 1904, the relief the Holy Family had promised her came.

Thresia had asked for permission to build a prayer house with three childhood friends in 1903, but approval would take ten years. In the meantime, freed from her three years of torture, she was a tireless nurse during a 1909 smallpox outbreak. She became a Carmelite tertiary the following year. But a public ministry of nourishing others spiritually and physically was to be her life's work. Approval to set up the prayer house finally was granted in 1913, and she and her friends founded the Congregation of the Holy Family the following year. Knowing her need for spiritual nourishment, her spiritual director set forth a daily schedule for the woman who at that point became known as Mother Mariam Thresia. It is said this schedule included only two fixed hours of sleep, with five hours set aside for meditations and penances.

In the next twelve years before Mother Mariam Thresia's death, the congregation made bold moves, going into areas previously considered off limits to women alone and ministering to the "untouchables," society's outcasts, as valued children of the Lord. They built convents, schools, hostels, an orphanage, and a study house, all focused on educating girls. Indeed, Mother Mariam Thresia, whose own formal education had been so limited, would come to be regarded as one of India's great educators and social reformers. She was beatified in 2000.

Mariam Thresia on Righteousness:
"From childhood my soul agonized with an intense desire to love God."[6]

BISHOP BOSCO PUTHUR ON MARIAM THRESIA:
"In the face of all adversities, Mother Mariam Thresia sought the will of God, relying on his grace, and embarking on a prayerful, penitent life. The story of the mother exhorts us to fulfill our life's mission in spite of all obstacles—unfaltered, optimistic, and ever relying on the grace of God."[7]

REFLECTIONS FOR YOU:

• For most of us, a regular spiritual schedule rather than catch as catch can is nourishing. Work with your spiritual director, a priest, or your prayer group to commit to setting aside a specific amount of time each day or each week to spend with the Lord.

• Most likely, you're not beset by demons in the way Mariam Thresia was. However, dark thoughts and fears can take up some of the space in our souls that belongs to the Lord. Think about talking during the sacrament of penance and reconciliation or in a pastoral counseling session about those spots and how you might be released from them.

• Three of Mariam Thresia's childhood friends stuck by her during her dark night of the soul and were the first members of the Congregation of the Holy Family. Offer your thanks, in person, on the phone, or in a note, to a friend who's been there for you in a time of trial.

• • • • • • • • • • • •
TERESA OF AVILA
March 28, 1515—October 4, 1582
Feast Day: October 15

If ever there a case of a near-miss of a woman saint when it comes to spiritual thirst—and fulfillment—it would be Teresa of Avila, whose writings on interior prayer were deemed so significant that she was named one of the first women doctors of the Catholic Church.

Teresa was by all accounts a beautiful, bright, outgoing, and altogether charming child and young woman. Her early life has a certain flavor of randomness to it: Her mother died when Teresa was fourteen. After that time, Teresa went to study with Augustinian nuns for eighteen months, returning home after she became sick. She then spent the next several years living with her wealthy father and her siblings or with other relatives. It was while she was staying with an uncle that Teresa decided to pursue a religious life, primarily it appears because it seemed to be a better option than the lives she had seen her mother and other female relatives lead.

She entered Avila's Carmelite Convent of the Incarnation just after her twentieth birthday, professed her vows two years later, then left the monastery the following year for health reasons that would culminate in a four-day coma in 1539. The issues were so severe that plans for her burial had begun; however, she awoke and returned to the convent, where she remained in the infirmary for three years.

The next eight or so years were a period of what Teresa referred to as wasting. Her prayer life was less than inspired. Her life at the convent was not what she had expected; she and the other sisters spent significant portions of the day chatting and gossiping in the parlor. The concept of cloistered life had for the most part been abandoned; some women left for weeks at a time, visiting friends and family. Teresa's vivaciousness made her a natural to chat up potential benefactors who came to visit. The vow of poverty was only laxly followed, with nuns holding on to property directly or indirectly. At one point, Teresa gave up prayer entirely, and returned to it only gradually and perhaps halfheartedly.

Thirst and hunger gushed forth during Lent 1554 when Teresa passed a crucifix on the way to prayer time. An entirely different, deeper relationship with Christ, including visions, verbal conversations, and other intense experiences followed. Her practice of mental prayer began in earnest.

But while Teresa was being fed internally, and was being prepared to feed generations to come through her writings on prayer, there was a more immediate ministry need: her sisters in the convent. In Teresa's opinion, it was time to return to the order's roots. In 1562, she received permission to found a Carmelite convent of thirteen women, less than a tenth the size of Incarnation's population. The sisters would wear sandals rather than shoes. Their habits would be made from rough wool rather than fine silk. They would lead a contemplative life in almost total silence, and they would exist in poverty, with no regular income from benefactors. This focus on God, Teresa believed, would help her sisters find fulfillment through prayer rather than through outside trappings.

Not surprisingly, this bold reformation was controversial. But support flowered. Between 1567 and 1576, eleven Discalced Carmelite convents were established. At one point, Teresa found herself back at Incarnation. An apostolic visitor sent by Pope Pius V had found serious disciplinary defects at the convent, and Teresa was dispatched there to restore order. With gentle guidance rather than combativeness, she managed to get the convent back on a path to spiritual righteousness.

Teresa's final years were beset by health issues and strife over the reform movement, including her denouncement (and eventual exoneration) by the Spanish Inquisition. At the end, she said, "O my Lord and my spouse, the hour I have longed for has come. It is time to meet one another."[8]

TERESA ON RIGHTEOUSNESS:
"May God give you fortitude so that you remain steadfast in righteousness, even if you find yourself surrounded by great danger. Blessed are trials when, however heavy, they do not make one turn aside in the least from righteousness."[9]

BLESSED PAUL VI ON TERESA:
"She strove with determination to tell the truth, to keep her word, to abide by her promises..."[10]

REFLECTIONS FOR YOU:
- What is your version of the Incarnation parlor room, full of frivolous chatter instead of devotion to the Lord? Maybe it's giggling with friends during the offertory or a boring homily. How can you reform your own spiritual life?
- It's easier to be the fun, popular person than the one who speaks up when a group situation—be it in our homes, our ministry, or our workplace—gets off track. What can you learn from Teresa's story to bolster your courage and faith to refocus the situation?
- Do you know someone who is going through a "wasting" period in his or her spiritual life? Gently ask if the person would like to talk about this dry time or, as Teresa's friend St. John of the Cross described it, "dark night of the soul." Listen. Pray. Don't offer solutions.

LEARNING MORE
You may be interested in learning more about righteousness in the journeys of these women:

- Maria Restituta (Helen Kafka), May 1, 1894—March 30, 1943. Maria wasn't one to stand by quietly when her faith or politics were being challenged. She opposed the Nazi annexation of Austria, where she had lived most of her life. She was working as a surgical nurse at the time, and when a new hospital wing was added, she placed crucifixes in every room. She refused to take them off the walls. Later, a Nazi doctor turned her into the Gestapo for circulating a satirical poem about Hitler. She spent the months in prison before her execution ministering to fellow inmates. Maria was beatified in 1998.
- Rose Philippine Duchesne, August 29, 1769—November 18, 1852. Many saints knew from childhood they had a vocation to take the Lord to those who had never heard their name. While Rose had contemplated a missionary's life early on, it was not until she was nearly fifty that the Religious Sisters of the Sacred Heart of Jesus had the opportunity to fulfill that call. She left France for the United States (specifically the St. Louis area) with four other sisters, and initially founded a school for the settlers' daughters. When she was in her seventies, she spent a year with a Potawatomi tribe in Kansas. While she did not know the language, the Potawatomi respected her presence greatly, calling her "woman who prays always."[11] Rose was canonized in 1988.
- Margaret Ball, 1515—1584. For Margaret's son Walter, converting to the Church of England was a matter of political expediency. It worked for him; he served as lord mayor of Dublin from 1580 to 1581. His mother had steadfastly refused to convert, and was known to harbor bishops and priests who came through the city. Even though Margaret was in her sixties

and suffered from physical ailments, one of Walter's first acts as lord mayor was to send her to prison in Dublin Castle. After his term was completed and his brother assumed the office, Walter still used his influence to keep Margaret incarcerated until her death. She was beatified in 1992.

- Monica, c. 331—387. Monica had an overpowering desire to help others discover their thirst for the Lord. Her constant evangelization resulted in the conversion of her husband and her mother-in-law. The most famous conversion she helped to facilitate was that of her son, Augustine of Hippo. His rejection of God estranged them for a time, but after Monica had a vision that his faith would be rekindled, she followed him from city to city and prayed for him without ceasing. She died soon after his baptism by St. Ambrose. Monica was canonized before institution of the Sacred Congregation for the Causes of Saints.

SUMMING IT UP AND TURNING IT OVER

Quenching one's thirst and hunger for the Lord can occur in any earthly venue, including ministering to those others consider "untouchable," as in Mariam Thresia and Laura's case. Teresa of Avila shows us that our own journey to fulfillment can provide guidance to our sisters and brothers in the form of writing or gentle guidance back to the straight path. From Hildegard, we learn that the political arena, used judiciously, can be the perfect place to share the Lord's message.

Lord, I thirst and hunger for your love. Help me to trust you will always be there to fill me up, and to help me share your Good News with others.

Chapter Five

MERCY

"Blessed are the merciful,
for they will receive mercy."
—MATTHEW 5:7

For Jesus himself said, "It is more blessed to give than to receive," Paul reminds the Ephesian elders in Acts 20:35. And nowhere can that call to give be more challenging than when it comes to mercifulness.

The *Catechism* identifies two types of works of mercy: corporal works, in which we assist those on society's margins or who are forgotten or ignored—the hungry, the homeless, the poor, the sick, and the imprisoned. The second type, spiritual works, is defined as "instructing, advising, consoling, comforting...forgiving and bearing wrongs patiently" (*CCC* 2447). Both types can come free and easy...or hard and challenging.

Let's start with the works of the body. Delivering canned goods for the parish food pantry or buying socks for distribution at the local homeless shelter are good works, there's no question of that. It requires a bit of a sacrifice of money and time to purchase the goods and deliver them. It can be harder to take that work a step further, and volunteer to help distribute the items and to look into the eyes and souls of the recipients. It can be harder still to hear the prison door clang behind you in jailhouse ministry or to bathe an aging parent or spouse no longer able to take care of himself or herself. It can be harder still to minister every day to people living and dying in the streets who have no one in the world but you and God to love them.

Similarly, it's good not to shake your fist at the woman who cut you off in traffic or to whisper with the person seated next to you at Mass about how awful the homily is. It can be harder to forgive the neighbor whose parties go on past midnight or the coworker who navigated her way into the position you so wanted by stabbing you in the back and taking credit that should rightfully be yours. It can be harder still to forgive the spouse who cheated on you or the texting teenager whose distracted driving killed your child or grandchild.

Whether it's a corporal or spiritual work, there's no quid pro quo here through which we offer mercy and then the recipient cries and tells us what great Christians we are. Often, our offering will be ignored, scoffed at, or denigrated. That doesn't matter. We offer mercy because we love God; we love the person no matter how appreciative or unappreciative he or she is of the offering; and we love ourselves. We offer mercy because God has given and continues to give it to us without reservation or limit.

That gift of showing mercy to society's forgotten people as well as to those who have wronged us is reflected in holy women including Teresa of Calcutta, Maria Karlowska, Frances Xavier Cabrini, and Elizabeth Canori Mora.

· · · · · · · · · · · · · · · ·

Teresa of Calcutta
August 26, 1910—September 5, 1997
Feast Day: September 5

Most of us know the story's basics: Mother Teresa, born Gonxha Agnes Bojaxhiu, grew up in what is now Macedonia and joined the Sisters of Loreto in Ireland when she was eighteen and prepared to become a missionary. She arrived in India about three months later and served as a schoolteacher until just before her thirty-sixth birthday when she heard what she termed a "call within a call"[1] that two years later would result in the founding of the Missionaries of the Charity Sisters, an order ministering to the poorest of the poor, initially in the slums of Calcutta. Their work was humble, simple, one on one. They went into homes, and also comforted those who were dying alone in the streets. They provided tender nursing care. They fed those who were starving. The stream of humanity they encountered was seemingly unending. But they just kept helping the next person, and the one after that, and the one after that, rather than focusing on the enormity and impossibility of their calling.

The order grew rapidly, eventually including more than six hundred orphanages, leper colonies, nursing homes, and clinics in more than a hundred countries, and its work brought Teresa much attention and acclaim, including the 1979 Nobel Peace Prize. Ironically, its founding roughly corresponded with the beginning of a dark night of the soul for Teresa, one that continued until her death. It was a deep spiritual drought, but she eventually came to see it as a blessing that her thirst for the Lord was not being quenched, much as Christ thirsted on the cross.

As so often happens when we are doing the best we can for the Lord, Teresa's leadership of the order and her life in general came under attack in this world. She said artificial contraception leads to abortion, and called abortion the greatest destroyer of love and peace in the world, which resulted in criticism that these views keep people impoverished. She encouraged baptism of the dying, which led some to say her ministry was more about converting people to Catholicism than about healing them. There were also allegations of poor medical care; chumminess with oppressive regimes in India, Haiti, and Albania; and incomplete financial disclosure.

Teresa had her defenders, as articulate as those who sought to tear her down. They responded that she was simply espousing the views of the Catholic Church, and that many of those who came to the sisters were dying and had no hope of healing, only of being treated with dignity and compassion in their final hours. As for her chumminess, it was noted Jesus dined with prostitutes and tax collectors.

What did Teresa say about all the allegations? It's said her response was something along the lines of "No matter who says what, you should accept it with a smile and do your own work." Except Teresa didn't say that, anymore than she said or wrote all kinds of other things we're told she said. In fact, the Mother Teresa of Calcutta Center has a whole list of lovely "Teresa" quotes that don't belong to her.[2] When it came to her critics, Teresa didn't go to a respected newspaper or magazine or news channel to refute them or come up with pithy aphorisms. No, she just kept on with those corporal works of mercy, helping one person, then another, then another. And if she thought much about her critics, perhaps it was during her prayer time, a time when for many years she heard nothing from the Lord. Perhaps she prayed for mercy for them as well.

TERESA ON MERCIFULNESS:
"God still loves the world and He sends you and me to be His love and His compassion to the poor."[3]

PRESIDENT RONALD REAGAN ON TERESA:

"Her charity goes out to all people. It knows no bounds. No bigotry—whether racial, religious, or political—can build barriers thick enough to keep out the pervasive warmth of her selfless benevolence."[4]

REFLECTIONS FOR YOU:

- Is there a corporal work of mercy you're avoiding out of pride or arrogance or fear? Talk with your parish's social services coordinator or a ministry representative about doing something that would open your heart and soul without alienating those who need help. If your heart is hard when it comes to women who have had abortions, consider writing thank-you notes for an organization such as Project Rachel that ministers to those seeking healing afterward.

- Are people questioning your motives for doing good? Perhaps it's a cranky teenage child or a jaded coworker. Just for today, greet them and their negativity with a smile and love. Journal about how you feel at the end of the day.

- Forgive someone for something you find unforgivable. Free up the room in your soul to love Jesus all the more.

. . . .

MARIA KARLOWSKA
September 4, 1865—March 24, 1935
Feast Day: June 6

Maria, the youngest of eleven children, was just seventeen when both of her parents died in what is today Poland's Pomeranian region. While the family had not been impoverished, Maria was determined to learn how make her way in the world and apprenticed as a seamstress in Berlin. Her course complete, she returned to work at her sister Wanda's sewing and embroidery shop.

Industrialization had come to the region and with it the arrival of many fresh-faced young men and women from the country looking for work. In some cases, the women instead ended up as prostitutes, often dying painful deaths from sexually transmitted diseases such as syphilis. It's said the first prostitute Maria personally encountered had just been taken into police custody, though she may have also first met the woman in her charitable work for the sick or at her sister's shop.

But unlike many in "proper" society, Maria didn't turn her back on the women. After all, the Lord had dined with prostitutes and tax collectors, so why wouldn't she? Her first works of mercy were spiritual: she listened to their stories, heard about their lives, and learned that they often were lacking in knowledge about the Lord. She determined that to get back on the right track, the women needed alternatives. It was Maria's prayer that those alternatives eventually would include a relationship with God, but she also knew they had to be able to support themselves financially.

In 1894, Maria founded the Sisters of the Good Shepherd of Divine Providence, and was among those who professed final vows in 1902. The local bishop gave final approval seven years later. In addition to the usual vows of poverty, chastity, and obedience, the sisters agreed to devote themselves to selfless work on behalf of those who were lost morally and took on the motto, "Search and save that which was lost." The original sisters wore habits Maria had designed and sewed. The sisters met the young women where they were—in brothels; hospital wards for those with sexually transmitted diseases; streets and alleys; and even in a cemetery. They gave them the messages of God's love and mercy, and of ways to build a better life.

Initially, Maria and some of the others took women into their own homes. With the congregation established, Maria found benefactors to help with the establishment of nine centers where the women lived and developed expertise in needlework, gardening, baking, and business skills. The sisters reflected the face of God in their corporal acts of mercy, training the women to do other work to support themselves. Medical care was provided for those with STDs. If a woman entered a center, she had to agree to stay there and complete the coursework. Mass and catechesis were available, but attendance was not required. Many chose to come, perhaps because Maria employed the same basic introduction to the Lord that she had as a child, teaching "prayers" to her dolls and the catechism to her nieces and nephews rather than judging them for their lack of knowledge. The women experienced the Lord's mercy in the respect they received.

The sisters' efforts were so successful that in 1928, Maria received the Gold Cross of Merit, Poland's highest civilian honor. She died seven years later.

The congregation continues to offer religious education and retreats today, and its roots in helping those on the fringes of society came back to the fore in the late 1980s and early 1990s as communism fell in Eastern Europe and economic upheaval resulted.

MARIA ON MERCIFULNESS:
"We must proclaim the heart of Jesus, that is, so to live from him, in him, and for him, as to become like him and that in our lives he may be more visible than we ourselves."[5]

ST. JOHN PAUL II ON MARIA:

"Maria Karlowska worked as a true Samaritan among women suffering great material and moral deprivation.... Her devotion to the Saviour's Sacred Heart bore fruit in a great love for people.... Thanks to this love she restored to many the light of Christ and helped them to regain their lost dignity."[6]

REFLECTIONS FOR YOU:

- While supplying food and shelter is important, our call to offer mercy doesn't end there. The next time you are providing physical assistance to someone (at a shelter, for example, or driving the person to a medical appointment), ask how things are going. Then listen, really listen.

- Maria began her way of service by teaching her dolls and her nieces and nephews about God. With a parent's permission, engage a child in a conversation about his or her view of the Father, Son, and the Holy Spirit or about one of the Ten Commandments. See how much you learn.

- Consider the sisters' motto: "Search and save that which was lost." How can you reflect that goal this week?

· · · · · · · · · · · · · · · · · ·

FRANCES XAVIER CABRINI

July 15, 1850—December 22, 1917

Feast Day: November 13

She wanted to be a missionary, to go to China and evangelize about the Lord's mercy. But no one thought too much about young Francesca Cabrini's dream. After all, she was a small, sickly child, born two months premature, the tenth of eleven children, only four of whom made it past adolescence. She was a good girl, a faithful girl, but those health problems concerned people who knew her. Maybe the problems also had something to do with that time she'd almost drowned, or that bout of smallpox. And so, Frances' bid to become a woman religious was turned down by several orders, including the one whose sisters had educated her in her teens.

When she was twenty-four, at her pastor's urging, Frances went to work at a troubled orphanage. When it closed six years later, she and friends she had met through that experience formed the Missionary Sisters of the Sacred Heart of Jesus. While in Rome to have the community's rule approved, her passion for missionary work touched Bishop Giovanni Battista Scalabrini, who was looking for a solution to a problem in an entirely different place than China. Some 10 percent of the Catholics in his Italian diocese had left for the United States, and the number was increasing. In the 1890s alone, 600,000 Italians would pass through Ellis Island. Bishop Scalabrini was concerned about the pastoral care they would receive in a country where the Church leadership was primarily of German and Irish descent, and so priests were being sent to the United States from Italy. He was aware the immigrants were in desperate need of corporal works of mercy, such as care for their orphans and elderly and sick. The small, frail woman whose heart was on fire seemed to be just the one to provide them.

Bishop Scalabrini had the ear of Pope Leo XIII on the matter, and when Frances returned for a private audience a few years later, she put before the pope her desire to go to China along with a letter the bishop had received from the archbishop of New York, Michael Corrigan, requesting the sisters to come there. The pope's response: "Not to the East, but to the West."[7]

Frances and six other sisters arrived in New York on March 31,

1889. Their reception was less than warm: Archbishop Corrigan urged them to return to Italy on the next sailing. The infrastructure wasn't set up; there was nowhere for them to stay, and their living stipend would not be available. But Frances informed him in no uncertain terms that she was staying put. She and the others spent their first night in a Lower East Side tenement so filthy that they chose to stay awake all night, singing and praying. The next day, they found lodging with the Sisters of Charity. They went door to door in the neighborhood, throwing themselves on the mercy of the other immigrants and asking for food and supplies. Finally, the archbishop acquiesced, and eventually gave Frances a frond from Palm Sunday as a peace offering. In the next dozen years, they would work well together, but challenge each other on ways in which the sisters' works of mercy would be expanded.

Frances never got to China, though her sisters did after her death. During her life, the frail woman who was afraid of the water crossed the ocean more than two dozen times and founded more than five dozen schools, orphanages, hospitals, and the like on three continents. In her final work of mercy, Frances was preparing Christmas candy for children when she died.

FRANCES ON MERCIFULNESS:
"I will go anywhere and do anything in order to communicate the love of Jesus to those who do not know him or have forgotten him."[8]

SISTER URSULA OF THE MISSIONARY SISTERS ON FRANCES:
"Hers was a life for God alone.... No task was too great, no labor was too hard, no journey too long and fatiguing, no sufferings were unbearable when the saving souls and succoring of suffering humanity were in question."[9]

REFLECTIONS FOR YOU:

- When she was young, people discounted Frances's zeal to be a missionary. Do you have an unrealized dream of service? It's never too late. How could you achieve it today?
- Frances had great instincts on when to take no for an answer—as with the pope—and when not to—as with Archbishop Corrigan. Where are you struggling with an authority's decision? Pray for the wisdom to accept it, or the strength to challenge it in a responsible way.
- Sometimes, what we want in the way we are to offer mercy to our brothers and sisters is not what the Lord desires, as Frances learned with her dream of China. Is there a place you are holding onto an old dream, rather than embracing the Lord's plan for you?

. . . .

ELIZABETH CANORI MORA
November 21, 1774—February 5, 1825
Feast Day: February 5

Sometimes, we offer mercy to people in faraway countries with whom we have almost nothing in common. Sometimes, we offer it to the destitute in our own country or neighborhood. And sometimes, perhaps hardest of all, we offer it to people in our own homes who may never reciprocate it in our lifetimes. The story of Elizabeth Canori Mora falls into this final category.

By all appearances, hers was a marriage with excellent prospects for success: Elizabeth came from a devout, once-wealthy family that had fallen on hard times. She and a sister spent part of their childhoods with the Augustinian sisters at a monastery. Christopher Mora was the son of a prominent Roman doctor. He became attracted to Elizabeth when she was nineteen, and they married when she was twenty-one.

Things started to fall apart after just a few months, and continued to disintegrate. Their first two children each died days after birth. Christopher took up with another woman. He neglected his law business, engaging in questionable practices, and instead focused on his mistress, gambling, and drinking. At home, things were even worse: he was verbally abusive to Elizabeth, and on at least one occasion, threatened her with a knife when he wanted her to sign a note saying it was all right for him to be with his mistress. The couple had two more daughters. Christopher's ways didn't change.

Almost everyone told Elizabeth to leave her husband—her parents, her friends, even her confessor. But she stayed. Was this degree of mercy really what the Lord had in mind? How could she see the face of God in his behavior?

The family's financial situation became so desperate that Christopher's parents told Elizabeth to downsize and move in with them. There, she was subjected to other abuse. Her sisters-in-law told her Christopher's problems were all Elizabeth's fault. He wouldn't be that way if he were married to someone else, they said.

Elizabeth took in sewing to make ends meet. She sold her jewelry, even her wedding gown. There was never enough. Yet somehow, she managed to set aside a little for the poor, and to do charitable works for those even worse off than she was. She did a lot of praying, especially for Christopher. She kept him involved in the lives of Marianna and Lucina, their daughters.

While Christopher's behavior didn't change, Elizabeth's life did. After a near-death experience in 1801 following the birth of one of their daughters, she began having mystical interactions with the Lord and his angels. She received revelations, and in 1807 became a Third Order Trinitarian. She struck up a friendship with another Trinitarian tertiary, Anna Maria Taigi, who was beatified in 1920. Strange as it may sound, among the people to whom Elizabeth offered mercy and counsel in that role were couples with troubled marriages. When she asked God for direction, he told her: "I desire you not to abandon these three souls, those of your husband and your two children, because I wish them to be saved by your means."[10]

In December 1824, Christopher came to visit his wife, who was gravely ill. "You will come back to God after my death; you will come back to God to give him glory,"[11] she told him.

Christopher wasn't there with the couple's two daughters when Elizabeth died two months later. But slowly but surely, the young women saw changes in their father, including his resumption of Mass attendance. Christopher expressed great remorse for the way he had conducted himself. He became a Third Order Trinitarian himself, and nine years after Elizabeth's death, a Franciscan priest. He died in 1845.

ELIZABETH ON MERCIFULNESS:

"Be diffident of your own weakness, and rely upon God, and you will see that all will be well."[12]

ST. JOHN PAUL II ON ELIZABETH:

"Elizabeth Canori Mora, amidst a great many marital difficulties, showed total fidelity to the commitment she had made in the sacrament of marriage and the responsibility stemming from it."[13]

REFLECTIONS FOR YOU:

- Say a kind word today to the person in your family you find most difficult to love. If that is dangerous, say a prayer for the person instead.
- Often, the people we dislike the most have qualities similar to ours, just magnified. Make a list of three positive attributes of the person who most works your nerves.
- Spend some time with a friend who's been married a long time. Without pressing for details, ask what practices or habits have helped his or her marriage stand the test of time.

LEARNING MORE

You may be interested in learning more about mercy in the journeys of these women:

- Gaetana Sterni, June 26, 1827—November 26, 1889. When she was sixteen, Gaetana married a widower with three children. She relished her role of motherhood, and became pregnant. But her husband died before the baby was born, and the child died soon after birth. Her in-laws at first prevented her from having much to do with the stepchildren. Gaetana briefly entered a convent, but left to care for some of her own siblings after her mother died. Rather than wearying of the caregiver role, Gaetana at twenty-six began a ministry of hospice care for the poor through the Sisters of the Divine Will. She was beatified in 2001.
- Mary Joseph Rossello, May 27, 1811—December 7, 1880. Mary Joseph yearned to be a nun. But her family was poor, and there was no money for a dowry. She worked for seven years, caring for an invalid, but the family valued her services so highly they were unwilling to provide the additional funds

she needed to become a sister. The situation was resolved when the local bishop bought a house and provided a couple of rooms for Mary Joseph to establish what would become the Daughters of Our Lady of Mercy to minister to underprivileged children. Remembering her early days, Mary Joseph insisted the Daughters never require a dowry from a prospective sister. She was canonized in 1949.

- Rosalie Rendu, September 9, 1786—February 7, 1856. What Mother Teresa was to those in the slums of Calcutta, Rosalie was to those in poverty-stricken areas of Paris for more than fifty years. As a Daughter of Charity, she established an orphanage, school, youth center, and other institutions. Similar to Teresa, Rosalie attracted attention from world leaders, including being honored with the Cross of the Legion of Honor by Emperor Napoleon III. She was beatified in 2003.

- Catherine of Genoa, c. 1447—September 15, 1510. Catherine's husband, Giuliano, sounds much like Christopher Mora. He spent money wildly, had a horrid temper, and was unfaithful. Catherine spent ten years in misery, and at one point prayed to be bedridden. A close encounter with God during confession ended her self-pitying attitude, and she began studying her faith intensely and volunteering at a hospital. Giuliano realized the error of his ways, and joined her in hospital ministry. Catherine was canonized in 1737.

Summing It Up and Turning It Over

The way we offer mercy can be big and impactful, as was the case with the missionary work of Mother Cabrini and Mother Teresa. We can see the face of God in the poor and underprivileged, as they did, and also recognize it in the challenges God sends us through his messengers. Mercy also can have a ripple effect when it plays out on a smaller stage, such as Maria's work with prostitutes and Elizabeth's decision to remain in her marriage and keep her philandering husband in her daughters' lives. Big or small, that's the thing about mercy: When we offer it, it comes back to bless us in more ways than we know.

Lord, help me to see your face in those I'm afraid to love because they look so different from me. Help me to show mercy to those in my life I find undeserving of it, because it's not my opinion that matters, but yours.

Chapter Six

PURITY

*"Blessed are the pure in heart,
for they will see God."*
—Matthew 5:8

Purity. It can be hard to find in today's culture of Internet pornography; immodest clothing, even for children; entertainers showing every inch of their bodies; and public figures of all persuasions using profane language with impunity.

And then there are those who are physically pure, who keep their private parts private and their mouths clear of bad language, yet cheat on their taxes, gossip about their neighbors, and find themselves too busy to provide any sort of assistance to those in need in their community or the world.

Clearly, pureness of heart is more than physical modesty or propriety. But what is it, exactly, and who has it? A child? A virgin? A cloistered religious? Maybe. Maybe not. The *Catechism* tells us that purity of heart "enables us to see *according to* God, to accept others as 'neighbors'; it lets us perceive the human body—ours and our neighbor's—as a temple of the Holy Spirit, a manifestation of divine beauty" (CCC 2519).

Purifying our hearts is a lifelong process. It gets easier the more we work at it, but it is always a struggle. And those times we fail in the struggle, rather than wallow in it, we serve and see God when we ask forgiveness and start anew. Consider David, arguably one of the greatest sinners of the Old Testament, who was so confident in God's love that even after having had an affair with his best friend's wife and sending his friend off to certain death in battle was brave enough to ask forgiveness and for the Lord to "create in me a clean heart, O God, and put a new and right spirit within me" (Psalm 51:10).

Cultivating a pure heart isn't about doing the right things for the wrong reasons—pride or arrogance, for example—or feeling bad about our sins after we commit them. It's about striving to do the right thing no matter how many times we've failed in the past so that we may move closer to the light. As our hearts are purified, it becomes easier and easier to see God: in people who don't dress or talk or look like us; in people who are in desperate need of our love and our care; in people who are cruel and even violent toward us; and yes, even in ourselves.

And, so, we resolve to seek the Lord's help in purifying our own hearts so that we might see his face, inspired by David's prayer and the lives of Katharine Drexel, Eurosia Fabris, Maria Goretti, and the Blessed Virgin Mary.

· · · · · · · · · · · · · · ·

KATHARINE DREXEL
November 26, 1858—March 3, 1955
Feast Day: March 3

It was a very comfortable life. The child known to friends and family as Kate or Kitty was born into the wealthy Philadelphia Drexel clan. Still, from an early age, she had good spiritual examples in her father, Francis, and her stepmother, Emma. Francis had a strong prayer life and contributed to a number of Catholic organizations and charitable institutions. Three days every week, those in need came to the Drexel home for food, clothing, and financial assistance. Katharine and her two sisters, one older, one younger, assisted with the distribution and taught Sunday school to some of the children.

Katharine gave some thought in her early teens to convent life, but decided against it, and not only on the advice of her parents and spiritual director. She wrote at the time: "I hate community life.... I'd hate never to be alone. I do not know how I could bear the privations of poverty of the religious life. I have never been deprived of luxuries."[1]

In January 1879, Katharine made her debut into Philadelphia society, a sign of the family's social standing. Later the same year, she learned that social standing and money couldn't protect one from all suffering. Her stepmother, the only mother she had ever known, found she had cancer. For the next three years, Katharine nursed Emma through her pain and suffering, and appeared to grow in faith as a result. It may have been the beginning of a purification process that would reap amazing rewards.

In February 1885, Francis died, leaving to his daughters the interest that would accrue from most of his $15.5 million estate. Katharine determined her philanthropic cause would be Native Americans, based on a mission visit in the Pacific Northwest. But she fell ill before she could begin in earnest on that effort, and went to Europe for healing. While there, she met with Pope Leo XIII and pleaded for missionaries to help the Native Americans. The pope's response was: "Why not, my child, yourself become a missionary?"[2]

A missionary? Katharine Drexel? Yes, it was true she'd considered a vocation, but as a philanthropic contemplative woman religious. And hadn't her own spiritual director said she could do more as a layperson? Perhaps this was a moment of purification of the heart for Katharine; after all, when you give money to the underprivileged, you're not in any physical or emotional danger. And if you help out personally from time to time, you can always go back to the comforts of your own home. You don't have to see those on society's margins as individuals and equals in God's eyes on a day in, day out basis.

Katharine's discernment continued. She and her sisters, who had charitable causes of their own, visited a number of reservations in the next three years, with Katharine contributing funds for schools, food, and clothing. Eventually, her spiritual director suggested she form a congregation to help Native Americans and African Americans. After a retreat, Katharine agreed. In February 1891, she took final vows with the Sisters of the Blessed Sacrament. She was thirty-two.

The next forty-five years were a dizzying time of establishing nearly five dozen schools and missions across the South, Southwest, and Midwest despite opposition by local residents and sometimes even members of the Church. Katharine shrugged off the threats, and kept on ministering until 1935 when she suffered a heart attack. She spent most of the next twenty years at the motherhouse in contemplation, "deprived" of that privacy and those luxuries she had been so concerned about when she was young and that she had learned were meaningless compared with the joy of seeing the face of God in ministry. Her monetary contributions as a sister are estimated at $20 million. Her spiritual contributions were priceless.

KATHARINE ON PURITY OF HEART:
"Divest your heart of all love of the world and of yourself and then you will leave room for Jesus."[3]

CARDINAL ANTHONY BEVILACQUA OF PHILADELPHIA ON
KATHARINE:

"Mother Katharine Drexel is great not because of her name or
her wealth, but because, like her Lord and Master, she served the
needs of all.... God was the center of her life; all she did radiated
from Him who kept her anchored in faithfulness and true to her
mission."[4]

REFLECTIONS FOR YOU:

• Contemplate Katharine's words about divesting your heart of
love of the world and yourself. What would it take for you to
do this? What is standing in your way?

• One of the secrets to seeing the face of God and purifying your
heart is humility, of being a servant rather than positioning
yourself as the "expert" at the local food pantry or homeless
shelter or in conversation with friends and family. Where are
you attempting to fill your own needs in ministry rather than
the needs of those you serve?

• Deprive yourself of one luxury this week. Maybe it's lunch
out, or a second cup of gourmet coffee. Put the savings in your
parish poor box anonymously. It may be a small amount, even
just a couple of dollars, but be confident it will be used to help
someone in need see the face of God.

• • • • • • • • • • • •
EUROSIA FABRIS
September 27, 1866—January 8, 1932
Feast Day: January 8

Sometimes, our purifying hearts show us the face of God in
people who look nothing like us, who don't speak our language
or dress like us or have the same color of skin. Sometimes, we

travel a continent or a world away for that spiritual awakening. And sometimes, we find it in our own neighborhood.

Eurosia Fabris's life was on the surface unremarkable. She was born on a farm in northeast Italy, and when she was four, the family moved to a nearby village. The village would be Eurosia's home for the rest of her life.

Family obligations meant her formal education was limited to two years of schooling. Still, in addition to her household tasks and outdoor chores, Eurosia found time to help her dressmaker mother and teach religious education at her parish. She also joined the Association of the Daughters of Mary, a lay organization for young women. It appears several young men of the village were smitten enough with Eurosia that they proposed marriage, but she turned them all down as she didn't feel that was the life she was called to.

Then, tragedy struck an area family in 1885. A young mother died, followed soon thereafter by a daughter, leaving behind two little girls under the age of two, one of them an infant. Their father, Carlo Barban, had his hands full, living in another town and caring for an uncle and a chronically ill grandfather and weighed down with debt incurred by his own father. What would become of the little girls, Chiara Angela and Italia?

For Eurosia, there was no question: She would care for them. Every day for six months, she went to the Barban home to mother the girls and do the housekeeping. At that point, Carlo was able to return home, and proposed marriage. Perhaps it was seeing the face of God reflected in those two babies. Perhaps the experience showed Eurosia she was indeed called to the vocation of wife and mother. In any event, she said yes—and took on her calling with gusto.

During their forty-four years of marriage, Eurosia would give birth to nine children, three of whom went on to become priests, including a son who wrote her biography. She and Carlo adopted a boy who became a friar, and took in an orphaned niece. Eurosia also served as a wet nurse for women in the area who were unable to breastfeed. Small wonder, then, that everyone called the woman Mamma Rosa. This unfailing love of children and community comes only from a purifying heart that saw her world according to God.

Eurosia's ministry wasn't limited to children. She tenderly nursed Carlo in the years before his death. She was a regular at religious education courses at her parish, participated frequently in Eucharistic Adoration, and was a secular Franciscan for twelve years. And despite managing a household with a dozen or more people coming in and going out at any given time, Eurosia provided for the poor with offerings from her kitchen or chicken coop and was known to allow people to live in the Barban barn. For Eurosia, as with the Lord, everyone was family.

EUROSIA ON PURITY OF HEART:
"The Lord loves us so much and died for us. Why be wary of his Providence?"[5]

ARCHBISHOP CESARE NOSIGLIA OF VICENZA ON EUROSIA:
"She accepted daily family life with all its troubles and sufferings, joys and hopes, in a continual search for God's will."[6]

REFLECTIONS FOR YOU:
• Money is tight for many of us today, just as it was for the Barbans. Without a financial commitment on your part, what can you do this week for someone in need?

- Eurosia's care for Chiara Angela and Italia is an example of living that second greatest commandment. Do you have a neighbor or friend who could use a little help, maybe an afternoon of babysitting or a dinner casserole or a ride to the grocery store?
- It's hard for many of us to even imagine managing a household with as many children as Eurosia did. Write a note of appreciation (or make a phone call) to a mother you know who seems overwhelmed.

• • • • • • • • • • • •

MARIA GORETTI
October 16, 1890—July 6, 1902
Feast Day: July 6

You likely know the basics of the Maria Goretti story, a story that exemplifies physical purity and the Catholic passion for preservation of human dignity. Maria, who was not quite twelve years old, was stabbed fourteen times with a dagger by a pornography-addicted young man. She managed to keep her virtue, but died the next day at the hospital. It's a stirring story of a strong child.

The background of the Goretti story adds texture to her martyrdom. The outcome exemplifies a confidence in the Lord... and defines purity of heart.

You see, Maria had a difficult life but focused on the Lord rather than her challenges. Poverty forced the Gorettis—Maria was the second oldest of five children at that time—to leave their farm in eastern Italy to move to the Roman countryside two hundred miles away. Rather than a fresh start, the relocation brought still more misery. Maria's father was unable to bring in the crops as he had pledged, and died of malaria in 1900. Her mother, Assunta, was forced to do field work to help satisfy the obligation, and a father and son moved into part of the family's living quarters. The father proved to be an alcoholic; the son, Alessandro Serenelli, recently returned from time at sea, spent his time looking at pornography and leering at Maria, who tended to her sisters and brothers and the house.

Maria's responsibilities prevented her from attending school. But she was able to make her First Communion due to a kind woman who taught her the catechism orally rather than through reading and writing. She also memorized prayers, and frequently said the rosary. Her purity of heart was evident even before the events of July 5, 1902, when Alessandro decided he had waited long enough for her as she sat mending one of his shirts.

Imagine knowing you were going to die and knowing who was responsible. Imagine looking that person in the eyes. Would you see the face of God in the fiend? Maria did. Before she died the day after the attack, she forgave Alessandro and said she'd see him in heaven.

The evidence was overwhelming. There was no question of the perpetrator's identity or motive. Since Alessandro wasn't yet twenty-one, he was sentenced to thirty years in prison rather than life. Initially, his heart and soul remained stone-cold. Then Maria appeared to him in a vision, offering him white lilies, the flower of purity. Slowly, over a period of eight years or so, he opened himself up to God. When he was released after twenty-seven years, he went to Maria's mother and asked for her forgiveness. She said she had to forgive him, as Maria did. Alessandro became a gardener and porter at a Capuchin monastery and lived quietly until his death in 1969. His will credited Maria as his light and protectress and expressed confidence he would see her and her mother in heaven.

There was one other significant day for Alessandro in the years after his release from prison. On June 24, 1950, Pope Pius XII canonized Maria. Assunta and Maria's four brothers and sisters were present in Rome. And somewhere in the crowd of jubilant, cheering thousands was Alessandro.

MARIA ON PURITY OF HEART:
"For the love of Jesus, I forgive (Alessandro)...and I want him to be with me in paradise."[7]

ST. JOHN PAUL II ON MARIA:
"Her spiritual life, the strength of her faith, her ability to forgive her murderer have placed her among the best-loved saints of the twentieth century."[8]

REFLECTIONS FOR YOU:
• Consider how freely Maria forgave Alessandro. Is there someone who injured you deeply? How can you see the face of God in that person? Make a list of the ways, even if the only one you can come up with is that he or she is or was a human being loved by the Father.

• Who have you wronged? How do the feelings around that incident continue to pollute your heart? Is there a safe way you can sincerely ask for pardon, even if it does not involve interacting with that person face-to-face?

• Our culture makes it difficult for children to remain children, pressuring them and their parents to adopt fashions and mannerisms far beyond their years. Consider writing a letter of protest to one of the manufacturers or marketers of particularly offensive music or clothing targeting preteens.

· · · · · · · · · · · · · · · · · ·

BLESSED VIRGIN MARY

First Century A.D.

Feast Day: Numerous, including three days of Holy Obligation
(Mary, Mother of God, January 1; the Assumption, August 15;
the Immaculate Conception, December 8)

Mary's moments in the New Testament are few, precious, and significant. Sometimes, she teaches by her actions. Other times, she teaches us by her seeming inaction.

Why would Mary, the mother of Jesus, born free of original sin, need to purify her heart? We venerate her Immaculate Heart to contemplate her love of God and the earthly journey on which he took her. What could we, normal, struggling children of God hope to learn from such a woman about purifying our own hearts? Ah, that's the thing about Mary. Like the family members and friends we most admire and desire to emulate, she shows strength in her vulnerability. Her lessons, while challenging, are as gentle as the shepherd we see in the Lord's face.

Consider the situations in which Mary finds herself. An angel appears to her, offering the Lord's greetings and calling her favored one. Mary doesn't immediately respond with "Hey, how are you and how's the Lord doing?" She doesn't run away either. Luke tells us she "was much perplexed by his words and pondered what sort of greeting this might be" (1:29). The angel explains God's plans for her, and she says yes. Surely, she can't know all that is to come. Still, she says yes, for she is confident in God's presence.

More amazement comes in the hours after Jesus's birth. She's doubtless tired and somewhat confused, far from the comfort of family and friends other than Joseph. Shepherds burst into the place where the family is staying, bringing stories of angels singing praise to the Lord about a newborn in a manger. Does Mary send them away? Does she burst into tears? Nope. She honors their experience and the effort they have made to come to Bethlehem: "Mary treasured all these words and pondered them in her heart" (Luke 2:19).

The face of God was presented to Mary in both those situations, in one by an angel, in the other by uneducated people who had little in material goods and may not have owned even their own flocks. Yet she recognized the Lord in both, carefully listening to his messengers, indifferent to the form in which they came.

Mary also teaches about purity of heart in two of her actions, one joyful and tinged with uncertainty, one sorrowful and tinged with hope. She, Jesus, and his disciples are in Cana for a wedding. Who doesn't like a wedding? The attendees are having such a good time that the wine runs out. Mary and Jesus exchange words about the situation, and he tells her his time has not yet come. But the Lord has placed something else on Mary's heart. She sees something that Jesus doesn't see, or perhaps doesn't want to see. The time *has* come. She tells the servants to do what her son says, and his public ministry begins.

That public ministry leads us to another example of Mary's purity of heart: the road to Calvary. She is there, unable to do a single thing to help her Son, who is bleeding, broken, struggling. She can't help carry the cross physically. As far as we know, she calls out no words of encouragement to him, no words of condemnation for his persecutors. She's just there, showing her face to Jesus every step of the way. It would have been easier for Mary to stay at home, surrounded by her friends or family members, where she could have broken down and grieved privately. Instead, she is God's face to Jesus—sorrowful, loving, faithful, hopeful that all the prophecies she has heard over the years from Elizabeth, from the angels, from Simeon, from Anna, from the shepherds and others will be borne out. She will continue to be that face as he is nailed to the cross, indeed up until the moment that Jesus hands her, the new Church, over to John, and hands John, the world of the faithful, over to her.

Full of grace, indeed. Pure of heart, certainly.

MARY ON BEING PURE IN HEART:

"My immaculate heart will be your refuge and the way that will lead you to God."[9] (Apparition at Fatima, June 13, 1917)

BLESSED TERESA OF CALCUTTA ON MARY AND BEING PURE IN HEART:

"Mary, my dearest mother, give me your heart so beautiful, so pure, so immaculate, your heart so full of love and humility, that I may receive Jesus in the Bread of Life, love him as you loved him and serve him in the distressing disguise of the poorest of the poor."[10]

REFLECTIONS FOR YOU:

• Say a rosary today. As you progress through the decades, put yourself in Mary's place. Ponder in your heart what she sorted through at each event, joyful, sorrowful, glorious, or luminous.

• Sometimes, we are too anxious about what's going to happen tomorrow, next week, or next year to ourselves or our loved ones. We go over our problems again and again in our heads or in conversations with others. Write down your biggest fear and ask for Mary's help in turning it over to her Son. Then put the note in the place you keep your clothes for the next season so that in a few months, you can see how that prayer was answered.

- Spend time this week learning more about the nearest Marian feast day. Contemplate Mary as a girl, being presented at the temple; as an older woman, at the time of the Assumption; or as a baby as the Immaculate Conception. What does she have in common at that time with you or a beloved relative or friend?

LEARNING MORE

You may be interested in learning more about pureness of heart in the journeys of these women:

- Maria Quattrocchi, June 24, 1884—August 26, 1965. Maria and her husband, Luigi, and their four children were a family devoted to faith—and love. One of their sons recalled growing up in a house of "'noisy joy'...with no religious excesses— or boredom."[11] Their home exemplified what the "domestic church" can look as we continually purify our hearts. They went to daily Mass and prayed the rosary nightly, and also enjoyed sports, vacations, and their second home in the country. In 2001, they became the first married couple to be beatified together.

- Maria Micaela of the Blessed Sacrament, January 1, 1809— August 25, 1865. Maria grew up in privileged circles. Her mother was a lady in waiting for the queen of Spain; and her brother served as her country's ambassador to France and Spain; and it is said she knew kings. Then, one day when she was thirty-five, she accompanied a friend to visit hospital patients suffering with sexually transmitted diseases. During the visit, Maria met a young woman raised in wealth who had turned to prostitution. The encounter galvanized Maria's will to help women regain their dignity, leading her to found a shelter and eventually a religious order. She was canonized in 1934.

- Anne-Marie Javouhey, November 11, 1779—July 15, 1851. Anne-Marie consecrated her life to the Lord on her nineteenth birthday, but failed attempts to join convents made some wonder if she'd heard God's plan for her correctly. Seven years later, she realized her vocation was to evangelize and serve enslaved people and founded the Sisters of St. Joseph of Cluny, traveling to Africa and the Caribbean. She was beatified in 1950.
- Agnes of Rome, c. 291—304. Agnes was just twelve or thirteen when she was beheaded for her refusal to sacrifice to the Roman gods. While there is no contemporary record, tradition holds that she was tortured in horrible ways, including being taken to a house of prostitution, but with the Lord's help maintained her virtue. Agnes was canonized before institution of the Sacred Congregation for the Causes of Saints.

SUMMING IT UP AND TURNING IT OVER

How do we become pure in heart? By obeying those two greatest commandments and respecting physical and spiritual purity, ours and that of others, and providing guidance and comfort to our brothers and sisters who have been robbed of it. It's about having the faith Mary did to ponder the incomprehensible in our hearts; the willingness Katherine had to get into the weeds of ministry; the example Eurosia's showed in loving the neighbors we can touch; and the belief in redemption Maria showed. These women's stories show us that with purifying hearts, we will indeed see the Lord's face however he chooses to present it to us.

Lord, I ask as your servant David did for a clean heart and a right spirit. Help me to value myself and my brothers and sisters as you do. Help me to see your face in all.

Chapter Seven

PEACEMAKING

"Blessed are the peacemakers,
for they will be called children of God."
—MATTHEW 5:9

We love peacemakers, in theory anyway. Think of all the poems and songs that have been written about the concept of peace over the millennia. In *City of God,* St. Augustine waxed poetically about peace in and between the body and soul; peace with God; and among people. "The peace of the whole universe is the tranquility of order," he concluded. "And order is the arrangement of like and unlike things in their proper place."[1]

That's the hard part, the finding in our hearts and souls while not compromising our faith, the proper places for those like and unlike things, whether they be people or views on politics or religion or how to fold the towels or make the bed. Order doesn't have to mean an authoritarian society. It does imply a sense of harmony and respect. Without it, we will never find peace.

In *The Violence of Love,* a collection of the writings of slain Archbishop Oscar Romero, tranquility again is used as part of peace's definition: "Peace is the generous, tranquil, contribution of all to the good of all. Peace is dynamism. Peace is generosity. It is right and it is duty."[2]

What did being a peacemaker look like in Jesus? We think of his last few days in earthly form. We think of his quiet surrender to the guards. We think of his admonishment to Peter for cutting off a guard's ear, and his healing of it. We think of his calm responses to the jesting Pilate's questions about who he is. We think of him on the cross, ignoring those who taunt him with questions about why he doesn't save himself.

As Jesus showed us, peacemakers aren't always loved or admired. We view their pacifism and equanimity and, yes, spiritual indifference to what happens in this world with suspicion and perhaps a little fear. How can they *not* raise their voices and denigrate those who oppose them? How can they *not* take advantage of every physical, mental, and emotional tool at their disposal to short-circuit the endless yammering and just get on with it? How can they *not* go along with the popular position because it's easy, and live to fight the good fight another day?

The answers are easy, though putting them into practice is so difficult. Because while those tactics may work in the short term, they're never successful in the long term. They don't change people's minds and hearts. That's why peacemakers respect the human dignity of those who do them harm. They know what they don't say or do can be as powerful as any words or actions. They are patient. They are confident in the Lord and the mission he has given them, whether it involves disharmony in their families, their country, their Church, and yes, even in themselves. They know God, not they nor those who are at odds with them, will define success.

And so, we look at the lives of four very different women— Dorothy Day, Catherine of Siena, Josephine Bakhita, and Elizabeth of Portugal—each of whom was a peacemaker in her own way.

. . . .

Dorothy Day
November 8, 1897—November 29, 1980

Jesus upset a lot of people in the establishment, well meaning or otherwise, in his thirty-three years in earthly form calling for peace and love. Dorothy Day had fifty more years than he did, and probably upset even more people during her time on this planet with her message of absolute pacifism, which she attributed to the Beatitudes, and her willingness to share the challenges and errors that led her to inner peace as a devoted Catholic.

The first public signs of her commitment to peace in the form of equality may have come in 1917, when she was arrested and spent fifteen days in jail for picketing at the White House for women's suffrage. At that time, Dorothy lived what was called a bohemian lifestyle; two years later, she became pregnant and had an abortion. She would later say of that time: "(The father) said that if I had the baby, he would leave me. I wanted the baby but I wanted Lionel more. So I had the abortion and I lost them both."[3]

Shortly thereafter, she was married civilly to another man; then, after that relationship ended and a new one began, she became pregnant again. It was a surprise; Dorothy had thought she was sterile after the abortion. It was during this time she began exploring Catholicism in earnest. Her daughter, Tamar Teresa, was born in March 1926 and was baptized in July 1927. Dorothy herself was baptized as a Catholic five months later.

While she was in Washington working on a story for *Commonweal* magazine, Dorothy visited the National Shrine of the Immaculate Conception and offered herself up for the workers of the world and the poor. That offering would be realized in public form on May 1, 1933, with the publication of the first issue of the *Catholic Worker* newspaper, sold for a penny a copy with no paid staff or advertising but plenty of advocacy journalism. Dorothy would remain its editor for the rest of her life.

The fortunes of the newspaper and of the Catholic Worker Movement, devoted to providing assistance to the poor and homeless and advocating nonviolent direct action on their behalf, would ebb and flow over the years. Support plummeted when the movement refused to support either side in the Spanish Civil War, and again suffered significantly for its continued stand of pacifism during World War II. Praising Cuba's Fidel Castro was another unpopular stand, and the movement's support of Cesar Chavez and opposition to the Vietnam War also had its critics.

And as for Dorothy herself, she would be imprisoned for nonviolent civil disobedience seven times, and shot at at least once. In the early 1940s, she became a Benedictine oblate. It was also about this time that she found herself turning to Thérèse of Lisieux and her Little Way, a spiritual style Dorothy had earlier discounted, indeed almost scoffed at. She spent more than five years at work on a biography of Thérèse that ultimately was published in 1960. In the book's preface, Dorothy wrote: "In these days of fear and trembling of what man has wrought on earth in destructiveness and hate, Thérèse is the saint we need."[4]

The Catholic Worker Movement goes on without Dorothy, as she would have expected and desired, in more than two hundred communities in the United States and abroad. The newspaper still costs a penny. As for Dorothy, she was declared a Servant of God in 2005, and in 2012, the U.S. Council of Catholic Bishops strongly endorsed the cause for her sainthood. The next step, assuming a document on her holiness and gifts meets with a commission's approval, would be a recommendation that she be declared Venerable.

DOROTHY ON PEACEMAKING:

"We do not yet know what it means. Loving our enemy.... We have great possessions, like the young man in the Gospel, and we turn from Christ to the use of force to protect them."[5]

CARDINAL JOHN O'CONNOR ON DOROTHY:

"Like so many saints of days gone by, she was an idealist in a non-ideal world. It was her contention that men and women should begin to live on earth the life they would one day lead in heaven, a life of peace and harmony."[6]

REFLECTIONS FOR YOU:

- What does it mean to love our enemies, as Jesus calls us to do? What one action can you take today to live the Gospel message? It may be something as simple and challenging as praying for someone whom you allow to disrupt peace in your heart.

- Spirituality is a journey. Revisit the life or writings of a saint whose heroic virtues you found less than inspiring when you were a teenager. What can this person teach you today in the same way Dorothy's view and understanding of Thérèse grew and deepened?

- Is there something in your past that you keep secret today not out of discretion, but out of shame? Perhaps it's a sexual assault or arrest or abortion or divorce. Make an appointment to discuss the situation with a priest or spiritual adviser.

. . . .

JOSEPHINE BAKHITA

C. 1869—February 8, 1947

Feast Day: February 8

They called her Bakhita, which means "fortunate." It was an odd name for the slave traders to have given the little girl, less than ten years old, who was so shaken by her kidnapping in the Darfur region of southern Sudan that she couldn't remember her own name. But Bakhita would prove to be the perfect name for this saint.

After locking her in darkness for weeks, the traders sold the child. She was then resold several times in the following years. Beatings and whippings were commonplace; the worst was the man who, when Bakhita was about thirteen, noted she had never been branded. His people took care of that for him, cutting her with a razor in excess of one hundred times on nearly every part of her body but her face, putting salt and flour in her wounds to ensure the sixty-plus patterns would not fade away.

Her next owner, Callisto Legnani, was different. Bakhita later remembered the Italian consul in Khartoum as the first owner who did not whip her. When she was about eighteen, he took her back to Italy with him and gave her to a friend, Augusto Michieli. Bakhita babysat the Michielis' daughter and together they attended the Canossian Sisters' Institute of Catechumens in Venice. Bakhita was drawn to the crucifix; it reminded her of her own suffering and wounds, and made her want to know more about Jesus.

In 1888, Michieli and his wife went to Africa for business reasons. During their absence, in 1890, Bakhita chose to be baptized and confirmed and took Josephine as her first name. As she grew in faith and understanding, she became more and more convinced that it was time to press for freedom. When the Michielis returned to Italy to take Josephine and their daughter back to Africa, she refused to go, with the support of the Canossians and the Venetian patriarch. A judge ruled in Josephine's favor, saying since slavery was illegal in Italy, she had been free since her arrival in 1885.

Rather than dwell on the injustices that had been her life for thirty-five years, Josephine made peace with her past. She formally entered the Canossian Sisters in 1893, made her vows three years later, and made a perpetual profession in 1927. Her assignments in religious life included being a convent greeter, sewing, and writing her memoir. It took her twenty years to complete the work, which was published in 1930. She achieved a degree of fame in Italy, traveling about to tell her story.

The slave traders had taken much from Josephine: her parents and six siblings, none of whom she ever saw again; her body; and her freedom. What they could not take was her human dignity and inner peace, and that wonder she had even as a child as she looked up at the sky and wondered how all this had come about. They might have laughed and sneered if they had known that when she talked of her kidnappers in later life, she said she was grateful to them, for without them, she would have never known Christ.

Josephine's kind of peacemaking is perhaps among the most difficult of all to achieve: her abandonment of serious past injustices so that she lived in the present—with her eyes on the glorious future promised in heaven.

JOSEPHINE ON PEACEMAKING:

"If I were to meet the slave traders who kidnapped me and even those who tortured me, I would kneel down and kiss their hands, for if that did not happen, I would not be a Christian and a religious today."[7]

JOSE LUIS LISALDE, SPANISH MISSIONARY JOURNAL EDITOR, ON JOSEPHINE:

"Bakhita taught us the path of liberation. The path she followed and that led her from slavery to freedom still has to be walked by so many people who are subject to a variety of forms of slavery."[8]

REFLECTIONS FOR YOU:

- Human trafficking continues today, not just in Africa but in our own country. Look into what you might do locally, through volunteering, writing letters, or donating supplies to those who seek to help bring to these victims the same peace Bakhita achieved.

- Who is disturbing your peace today? Perhaps it's an estranged spouse or friend. Spend some prayer time blessing him or her and liberating yourself emotionally and spiritually from the person's bondage.

- With a friend, read *Spe Salvi* (Saved in Hope), Benedict XVI's 2007 encyclical that includes references to Bakhita. Discuss Benedict's challenge near the end: "As Christians, we should never limit ourselves to asking: how can I save myself? We should also ask: what can I do in order that others may be saved and that for them too the star of hope may rise?"[9]

. . . .

CATHERINE OF SIENA
March 25, 1347—April 29, 1380
Feast Day: April 29

Catherine of Siena was a sort of minister without portfolio. While she with one exception never held a formal position at court, in government, or in the Church other than as a lay Dominican, her political advocacy skills were formidable. Catherine is credited with playing a significant role in fostering peace among the Italian city-states in the fourteenth century. (Areas of northern and central Italy at that time, rather than being united in a single nation, were governed locally as municipalities or regional areas, and fighting and disputes were common.) There is evidence she also had a part in the return of the papacy to Rome in 1377 after nearly seventy years in France.

How did a woman who likely didn't learn to read until she desired to learn the Divine Office and who didn't learn to write until she was thirty accomplish all this?

From an early age, Catherine exhibited negotiation skills. The twenty-third child in her family, it was decided when she was sixteen that she would marry the widower of an older sister. Catherine knew the man to be a less-than-ideal husband. She refused. Her parents insisted. She went on a fast. Her parents still insisted. She cut off her long hair to make herself less attractive. Finally, her parents gave in, allowing her instead to become a lay Dominican. That took negotiation as well; in those days, widows and matrons became tertiaries, not attractive young single women. Initially, Catherine spoke only to her confessor and left the house only for Mass. Guided by God, she was doing what she would later counsel others to do: build a cell inside her mind.

That concept, of a mental place to which one could retreat from the world, would have been a foreign concept to most of Catherine's contemporaries. In the mid-fourteenth century, during her formative years, they were focused on survival. From 1346 to 1353, the Black Death laid waste to Europe. Between 1348 and 1350 alone, it's estimated that a third of the world's population between Iceland and India succumbed. The blame often mistakenly fell on Jews, bad air, or God's wrath.

After three years of virtual solitude, Catherine had a mystical encounter with Christ in which she was told to reenter the world. Her public ministry began with nursing during another epidemic, and ministering to prisoners and those about to face execution. Her style began to draw followers, and her fame spread. After being called to Florence for reasons that are not entirely clear, she began dictating letters that called for peace within the city-states and for the pope's return, primarily to instigate clerical reform. The priestly population had been devastated by Black Death, and those who remained were viewed as lax in adhering to their vows of obedience and chastity.

More than three hundred of Catherine's letters to the pope survive. She also wrote to military leaders, monarchs, and private citizens. In many cases, the God she showed them, the God who had made himself known to her through mysticism, was a different God from the one they knew from the Black Death or the time's worldview. Catherine showed them a loving God who desires good for us and wants to talk with us through prayer, not a God who expects unremitting sacrifice. These writings are responsible for her selection as a doctor of the Catholic Church. And perhaps that peacemaking, between her contemporaries and the Lord, was her greatest accomplishment of all.

CATHERINE ON PEACEMAKING:
"Everything comes from love, all is ordained for the salvation of man, God does nothing without this goal in mind."[10]

BENEDICT XVI ON CATHERINE:
"The century in which she lived...was a troubled period in the life of the Church and throughout the social context of Italy and Europe. Yet, even in the most difficult times, the Lord does not cease to bless his People, bringing forth Saints who give a jolt to minds and hearts, provoking conversion and renewal."[11]

REFLECTIONS FOR YOU:
• What are you afraid to take to God? Reread Catherine's statement about God's love. Talk with your confessor or spiritual director about your fear.

- Catherine relied on her friends and followers to carry her words via letter to others. Write a thank-you note today to a friend who helps you with something you are unable to do yourself.
- Catherine pushed the pope to get the priesthood back to the basics. Who among those in the ordained or consecrated life inspires you with his or her humility and pastoral care of community? Write that person a thank-you note as well.

. . . .

ELIZABETH OF PORTUGAL
C. 1271—July 4, 1336
Feast Day: July 4

If Elizabeth of Portugal were alive today, she would probably be on one of those lists of the world's most admired women. Without any governmental title beyond queen, she was a peacemaker among the various rulers in her extended family in Spain and Portugal. In addition, her strong faith gave her the confidence and serenity to endure her husband's philandering and keep the peace at home, channeling her energies to reflect the Lord in her service to the poor.

As part of a strategic political alliance, Elizabeth, a Spanish princess who was said to be beautiful, was married at a young age to King Denis of Portugal, about eight years her senior. It appears eight years passed before they had their first child, Constanza; a son who would become Afonso IV was born a year later, when Elizabeth was about twenty. Denis, while regarded as an excellent ruler, was a less than ideal husband. He's believed to have had as many as nine children with other women, including another son who also was named Afonso whom he favored.

Elizabeth did not allow herself to become embittered by her husband's infidelity. There is no record of her ever reproaching him or complaining about him publicly. Rather, she continued to treat Denis with kindness and respect, cared for some of his children with other women, and forged her own path. She is credited with a role in the 1297 Treaty of Alcañices, which headed off a war between Portugal and Castile and set territory boundaries that still exist to this day. (As was common at that time, it also committed to spouses for Elizabeth's and Denis's two children.) A few years later, her peacemaking skills resulted in an alliance between Castile and Aragon, both ruled by relatives.

Learned in Latin, Elizabeth had a faith life that included working to establish the Feast of the Immaculate Conception, still in its nascent days, in the city of Coimbra. She built a convent for the Poor Clares, and a dwelling next door for herself. Elizabeth also was tireless in her work for the underprivileged, establishing an orphanage, hospice care for the poor, and a hospital. She was something of an architect, far more involved in the design of these structures than most royalty.

Eventually, the ill will between Denis and their son threatened to erupt into full-blown war. Initially, Denis thought Elizabeth was among those who urged on Afonso, and refused to let her venture out beyond the city walls. Even though some of her son's supporters offered to help her, she obeyed her husband's order until he realized he was wrong. When Elizabeth heard the fighting was escalating to a particularly dangerous level, she went out to the battlefield, several days' journey on a mule, and brokered the peace between them in 1324. In the following year, Denis's health declined significantly; she didn't leave his side except to go to daily Mass until his death in 1325.

Elizabeth then became a Franciscan tertiary and moved into

the house she had built next to the Poor Clares. She founded a hospital and named it after her great-aunt, St. Elizabeth of Hungary, another Third Order Franciscan. In the year before her death, another family battle erupted; Afonso, who was then king, felt his daughter Maria's husband, the King of Castile, had treated Maria badly and fighting had begun. Again, it was Elizabeth who brought peace to the family and the region. She died shortly thereafter.

ELIZABETH ON PEACEMAKING:
"God made me queen so that I may serve others."[12]

KING DENIS ON ELIZABETH:
"...God made you without peer in goodness of heart and goodness of speech, nor is your equal anywhere to be found..."[13]

REFLECTIONS FOR YOU:
- Without meddling, is there a way you can help to resolve a family misunderstanding? Perhaps you could offer your home as a neutral territory for the estranged parties to meet for coffee or dinner.
- In part of your world, you are surely "queen": within your family, among your friends, in your parish or neighborhood, or at work. Consider Elizabeth's words. What can you do in that situation to better serve others? Provide a kind word or smile? Refrain from gossip or thoughtless comments? Offer to help with a task or chore? Be regal in your service.
- King Denis wasn't a bad ruler, but his impulses and lack of self-control had to have hurt Elizabeth deeply, despite her best efforts to be spiritually indifferent and focus on service. Apologize to someone whom you have hurt by being self-absorbed, and pray for guidance in how you can keep this from happening again.

LEARNING MORE

You may be interested in learning more about these women as peacemakers:

- Liduina Meneguzzi, September 12, 1901—December 2, 1941. At twenty-five, the Italian-born Liduina became part of the Sisters Congregation of St. Francis de Sales, working as a boarding school nurse. About ten years later, she became a missionary in Ethiopia. There, Liduina became known as "the ecumenical flame" for the respect and care with which she ministered to all—Muslims, Catholics, Copts, and nonbelievers—she encountered while working at a military hospital for the next four years before her death. She was beatified in 2002.

- Thérèse Couderc, February 1, 1805—September 26, 1885. Thérèse thought she would be a teacher when she joined France's Sisters of St. Regis. But the number of visitors to the shrine of St. Regis swelled to the point that Thérèse saw the need for a retreat house. Internal disputes about finances and other issues ensued, and Therese found herself no longer the superior, assigned to the most humbling and lowest of tasks. She accepted the demotion rather than engage in a battle. She was canonized in 1970.

- Zdislava of Lemberk, c. 1220—1252. Zdislava shows us peace begins at home—if our family understands it. Zdislava had initially planned to become a hermit, but eventually married a Czech nobleman. She and her husband were at odds over her charitable efforts, especially among Eastern Europeans who fled their homes during the Tatar invasions. It is said that her husband finally had had enough of the situation, and decided to remove one of the people for whom Zdislava had provided lodging. In place of a man or woman, he found a crucifix. He then embraced her ministry. She was canonized in 1995.

- Genevieve of Paris, c. 422—500. Genevieve's story shows us the power of prayer—and the power of a single person who believes in prayer. It is said that when the Huns threatened Paris in 451, she told people the city could be spared by prayer. Some laughed at her, and even threatened to stone her. But Genevieve convinced a group of women to join her in prayer and fasting. And indeed, the invaders turned away from the city. Genevieve was canonized before institution of the Sacred Congregation for the Causes of Saints.

Summing It Up and Turning It Over

Peace is about more than being at a bargaining table. It's about letting go of past hurts in Christ's name and opening ourselves again and again to the potential of unity. We learn this from Dorothy's willingness to be arrested time and again in the interests of advancing justice for all; Josephine Bakhita's stunning ability to forgive those who took her from her family; Elizabeth's selfless efforts to create harmony within her region and her family; and Catherine of Siena's service as a vessel for God to be reconciled to his people in the aftermath of the Black Death.

Lord, let me never be too proud or too fearful to seek to advocate for peace.

Chapter Eight

PERSECUTION

"Blessed are those who are persecuted for righteousness' sake,
for theirs is the kingdom of heaven.
Blessed are you when people revile and persecute you and utter
all kinds of evil against you falsely on my account."
—Matthew 5:10—11

Following Christ sounds so easy on the surface: love the Lord, your neighbor, and yourself unceasingly. But it is the hardest thing we will ever do, because no matter how meek and peaceful and poor in spirit we are, evil in the world will seek to take us off the narrow path.

Evil and its companion, persecution, come in different forms. Sometimes, it's a person in a uniform, telling us to stop talking about Jesus or be killed. Sometimes, it's a person who's mentally disturbed. Sometimes, it's an authority figure who is fearful or mistrustful of the way our relationship with the Lord manifests itself. And sometimes, and this is perhaps the most difficult to accept, it's a relative or friend whom we love or once loved with all our hearts and souls.

In some cases, persecution in Christ's name is easy to identify, because our persecutors tell us that's why we're being physically tortured, why we're being separated from all we value on earth. Other times, the Lord is there, but not as front and center, such as when we make a stand for the oppressed, for justice, for truth, for righteousness.

Persecution knows our weak points. Which is easier, to die a quick, martyr's death before a firing squad or on the executioner's block...or to trudge on for thirty-nine years, not allowed to say a word to anyone other than our confessor? Which is easier, to suffer the pain that so often accompanies a final illness...or to be shunned by the popular crowd in the neighborhood or at work? You can bet that the form that makes us the most vulnerable is the one that persecution will choose.

But in ways it never intended, persecution can be our friend. It makes us step up and do heroic things in Christ's name where otherwise we might have lived a quiet, placid, safe life. It makes us set aside our pride and arrogance. It strips us bare of our greed and earthly possessions. It can take away everything we have—except faith. It cannot separate us from God, not if we don't allow it to.

Sára Salkaházi, Mary of the Cross MacKillop, Laura Vicuña, and Lucy of Narni lived worlds apart and spoke different languages. Sometimes they spoke up against the way in which they were being persecuted; sometimes they held it in the silence of their hearts. We can learn from the grace with which each of them bore their cross.

· · · · · · · · · · · · ·

Sára Salkaházi
May 11, 1899—December 27, 1944
Feast Day: December 27

Sára Salkaházi was nothing like the stereotypical martyr—or woman religious, for that matter. When she was young, she smoked. In her twenties, she liked hanging out in post-World War I cafes and enjoyed Romani music. In her youth, she was described as a tomboy; throughout her life, those who knew her described her as strong willed. And that strong will combined with her strong faith allowed her to offer up her life two days after Christmas as World War II began to wind to its conclusion.

She was born Sára Schalkház in what is now Slovakia as the second of three children whose father died when she was just two years old. Her young adult years were a time of searching; she studied to be a teacher, but taught in a classroom for just a year. Her other jobs included apprenticing as a book binder and working in a shop where women's hats were sold. She was engaged for a time, then broke it off. Sára was also a writer whose first professional newspaper article was published before she was twenty, and that would open doors to her strong bent for social justice. She wrote about the poor and inequity as the editor of the national Christian Socialist Party of Czechoslovakia's newspaper, and also sat on the organization's governing board.

When she turned thirty, Sára could no longer ignore the Lord's tugging at her heart, and entered the Society of the Sisters of Social Service. She threw herself into her initial assignments—working for Catholic Charities, editing a publication, organizing disparate organizations into a national Catholic women's association. She neared exhaustion, to the point that the sisters were concerned about her and did not allow her to profess her final vows until 1940.

By that time, Sára had given serious thought to missionary work in Brazil, but decided against it given the tumult that World War II brought. It wasn't as if there wasn't plenty to keep her busy in Hungary. In 1941, she was named national director of the Hungarian Catholic Working Women's Movement, an organization of more than ten thousand members across fifteen dioceses. She wrote a play about St. Margaret of Hungary, who had been canonized in 1943. It had one performance before the Germans overran the country in 1944. Sára had already made public in 1943 her disgust with the Nazis, changing her last name to the more Hungarian Salkaházi. In private, she was channeling her efforts to help those hated by the Nazis and their aligned Hungarian Arrow Cross Party: besides worker schools, children's soup kitchens, and senior citizens' residences, Sára was responsible for hostels for single working women. In those hostels, she was also hiding about one hundred Jews.

On the morning of December 27, 1944, Sára gave a meditation on martyrdom. It was just hours later that she and another sister were walking toward one of the hostels, and saw Arrow Cross police were onsite. Sára could have kept walking and returned to the hostel after they left. Instead, she stepped forward and identified herself as the leader. She was arrested along with five others, four Jews and an instructor. They were taken to the Danube River, stripped, and shot. Eyewitnesses said Sára made the Sign of the Cross just before her death.

SÁRA ON PERSECUTION:

"Have a desire for martyrdom; if, out of God's special love you would not get it, at least live the martyrdom of sainthood!"[1]

AN EYEWITNESS TO SÁRA'S ARREST:

"She knelt down on one knee, and the light of the vigil light shone into her face.... A few seconds later, one of the grim-looking Arrow Cross men seized her and shouted: 'Come on! During the night you will have enough time to pray!' She stood up, but her face radiated such peace that it seemed like a kind of miracle...."[2]

REFLECTIONS FOR YOU:

- Sára's moment came when she didn't keep walking by the house. The Blessed Virgin's moment came when she said yes to the Lord. Pray that you will respond as the Lord desires when your next moment comes.

- It's not safe to be a Christian in much of the world today. Consider sending a donation to Catholic Relief Services, or visit the CRS virtual chapel online to offer a prayer request.

- Many of us are like Sára in that we have many, many projects going at once. Commit to carving out an hour sometime this week from your busy schedule to spend time at an adoration chapel or another quiet place listening to the Lord.

. . . .

MARY OF THE CROSS MACKILLOP
January 15, 1842—August 8, 1909
Feast Day: August 8

Persecution sometimes enters our lives indirectly. We may not be the actual target, but it's convenient to punish or disparage us to get to the real target. It's then that we must discern whether we submit to or challenge the effort. For much of her life, St. Mary of the Cross MacKillop chose the latter course—and ultimately prevailed.

Mary was the first of eight children born to Scots immigrants to Australia. While the family was loving, her father was a poor businessman and suffered many financial challenges. By the time she was fourteen, Mary was often the primary breadwinner, working at a stationery store in Melbourne. At eighteen, she became the governess to some cousins, and met Fr. Julian Tenison-Woods, who became her spiritual director and would be intertwined in her life for years to come. The priest was extremely concerned about the education of children in south Australia, and when Mary was twenty-four, she, a sister, and other women began teaching, dressed as religious postulants, at a school one of her brothers had helped transform from a stable. The following year, Mary became the first sister and mother superior of the Sisters of St. Joseph of the Sacred Heart. The sisters became known as the "Brown Joeys" because of their habits. Anyone could attend their school, whether or not tuition could be paid. When Mary took her final vows in December 1869, the sisters numbered seventy-two, operating more than twenty schools and other services.

Things became difficult while Mary and a group of sisters spent extended time in Brisbane. When they returned to Adelaide, some of the sisters and area priests expressed grave concerns about Fr. Tenison-Woods's ability to lead the congregation, citing exhaustion and mental problems. There also was concern about possible pedophilia by a priest at a nearby parish, allegations Fr. Tenison-Woods had reported. The overall situation was so severe that Bishop Laurence Shiel ordered a commission to investigate, and the group's recommendations included giving local priests authority over each community. Mary challenged the finding via a letter to the bishop, and was promptly excommunicated on September 22, 1871, for insubordination. The action was lifted five months later, shortly before the bishop's death. Also in 1871, Church authorities began plans to relocate Fr. Tenison-Woods; he eventually settled in Brisbane in 1874, where he founded another order.

For her part, Mary went to Rome in 1873 to seek the pope's approval for the Sisters of St. Joseph. While it was agreed the superior general and council would have authority over the order and Pope Pius IX encouraged the sisters' work (though he referred to Mary as "the excommunicated one"[3]), final approval of the order was not immediately granted and Mary accepted this. This did, however, create a strain in Mary's relationship with Fr. Tenison-Woods, though she always gave him credit for founding the Sisters of St. Joseph.

Mary returned to Australia two years later, only to find continued friction with some of the local bishops. Sisters were removed from two dioceses as a result. Another official visitation occurred in 1883 over concerns including the society's debt and allegations that proved to be unfounded about Mary's use of alcohol. While the matter ultimately was resolved for the most part in favor of the society, it was determined Mary would no longer be superior general. She was succeeded by Mother Bernard Walsh, and the two worked well together until Mother Bernard's death in 1898 while Mary was in New Zealand. In the first election in seventeen years, Mary was reinstated as superior general.

A stroke permanently disabled Mary in 1901, but the congregation reelected her as its leader nonetheless. In 2009, the centenary year of Mary's death, the archbishop of Adelaide apologized to the sisters for her brief excommunication.

MARY ON PERSECUTION:
"The cross is my portion—it is also my sweet rest and support."[4]

CARDINAL GEORGE PELL ON MARY:
"Hers is an Australian voice, the voice of a great woman all Australians can recognize as one of their own. But her example

and teachings—about forgiveness, about resisting hardness of heard, and about working to overcome evil, refusing to be disheartened or defeated by it—speak to women and men well beyond our shores and in all ages."[5]

REFLECTIONS FOR YOU:

- Like Mary and Fr. Tenison-Woods, we all have friendships that have not ended well. Offer up some forgiveness for the person today, even if he or she is not receptive to it.
- There is no indication Mary was ever less than respectful to the priests, bishops, and cardinals with whom she had disputes. What strength can her example provide in a similar situation in your life?
- Pray for those who have been excommunicated and those who found it necessary to issue such a sanction, that in the name of Christ a positive resolution may be effected.

· · · · · · · · · · · ·

LAURA VICUÑA

April 5, 1891—January 22, 1904

Feast Day: January 22

Laura found herself in a desperate, some might say no-win situation, of threats, evil, and persecution. Her mother had been in a similar predicament. But although Laura was not yet thirteen, her response was quite different.

The child was born in Santiago, Chile, to an unlikely marriage. Her father, Joseph Domenico Vicuña, came from the aristocratic class. Her mother, Mercedes, came from humbler beginnings and was never really accepted by her in-laws. Civil war in the year of Laura's birth caused the family to relocate four hundred miles south. Another daughter, Julia Amandina, was born eighteen months after Laura. Then, Joseph died suddenly, leaving Mercedes with few resources.

The little family moved to neighboring Argentina, where Mercedes encountered a man described variously as a gaucho (cowboy or perhaps rancher) or the owner of low-cost lodging. His name was Manuel Mora, and he took a liking to Mercedes. With few options available to her, Mercedes agreed to be his woman and to work for him if he paid for the girls' education at a boarding school twenty miles away run by the Salesian Sisters.

Relatively early on, Laura realized that her mother was not in a right relationship. Mora's evilness was apparent in the way he abused his slaves and animals. The child prayed daily for her mother to leave him. Laura became so dedicated to her prayers and to the Salesian way that she asked if she could become a sister. She was advised to wait just a bit.

On the occasions Laura came home from school, her mother asked her to pray in secret, where Mora couldn't see her. When Mora made sexual advances toward the girl and she resisted, he refused to pay her tuition. The sisters then gave her a scholarship so she could remain at the school. At one point when she was home for vacation, Laura refused to dance with Mora at a festival. He proceeded to tie her mother to a post and publicly whip her.

Laura's health went downhill after she became caught in a severe rainstorm in July 1903; eventually, it was determined she had pulmonary tuberculosis. She came home ill late that year, and Mercedes moved her family into town. Mora came to demand that they return; when Laura refused, he beat her severely. While she regained consciousness, it became clear that she would not survive. She died eight days later, but not until after she told her mother she was offering her life for her and begged her to repent. Mercedes then at great risk to herself managed to escape her persecution and return to Chile. She died there in 1929. Amandina remained in Argentina and married. As for Mora, he died in a fight over a horse race.

Laura was beatified in 1988. Two years later, the Salesian sisters and others in the Philippines founded the Laura Vicuña Foundation to help as many as 1.5 million street children in that country.

LAURA ON PERSECUTION:
"Suffer silently. Smile always."[6]

PROFESSOR JOHN CUSSEN ON LAURA:
"Her story speaks to themes other than chastity's worth—to issues of caste and social status, to the contest between civilization and barbarism, to the plight of peasant mestiza women in the early modern era, and to the assertion of women's rights and roles in the same era..."[7]

REFLECTIONS FOR YOU:
- Desperate times can lead us off the Lord's path. Do you know someone whose life is less than Christlike due to poverty or illness? Without passing judgment, offer to help him or her look into resources that might be available through your parish, Catholic Charities, or government agencies.
- Laura's mother asked her not to pray when Mora was around because she knew it would upset him, and she stopped participating in the sacraments. Is something keeping you from regular Mass attendance? Consider making an appointment for pastoral counseling to discuss this separation.

- While Laura advised suffering silently, she spoke volumes by her actions—by refusing to go along with Mora, by encouraging her mother to leave him, by praying for her mother's conversion and bravery. Talk with one of your children (or grandchildren or other child, with a parent's permission) about when speaking up against persecution is the right thing to do, and how to do it.

. . . .
LUCIA BROCADELLI (LUCY OF NARNI)
December 13, 1476—November 15, 1544
Feast Day: November 16

When you hear the words Lucy and Narni, you may think of Lucy, the youngest of the Pevensie children in C.S. Lewis's Chronicles of Narnia series. Lucy sees things other people don't. At the end of the series, by then known as Queen Lucy the Valiant, she is among the children who stay in "real" Narnia because back in their own world, they have died in a train accident.

There really *was* a Lucy of Narni, Lucia Brocadelli, and C.S. Lewis may or may not have had her in mind when he created the Lucy Pevensie character. But Lucia Brocadelli's path was much different from Lucy Pevensie's, and included half a lifetime of what some would call penance and others would call persecution.

The oldest of eleven children, Lucy of Narni had a vision of the Virgin Mary when she was just five. She desired to become a nun but after her father died when Lucy was thirteen, an uncle was determined she would wed. Prospect after prospect fell by the wayside because of Lucy's vow of perpetual virginity. In 1491, a count named Pietro agreed to marriage on her terms.

While he showed patience for some time, Pietro eventually tired of the situation and of Lucy's visions and ordered her confinement for most of Lent in 1494. On Easter, she managed to get out and returned to her mother's home. After about a month, she became a Dominican tertiary, a move that angered Pietro so much that he burned down the monastery that had accepted her. Lucy then remained with her mother until 1495, when she moved to Rome and joined a monastery there.

Accounts of the next ten years vary, but it's safe to say that Lucy was the talk of Italian Catholic circles. She was sent to Viterbo to open a new convent and, while living there during Holy Week in 1496, experienced the stigmata. Some say for the three years she was in Viterbo, observers could see a loss of blood each Wednesday and Friday. Close to a half dozen inspections, including one by the pope's physician, validated the presence of her wounds. People came to see her often, and in some cases asked if she could go into an ecstasy for them.

Accounts of Lucy's gifts caught the attention of Duke Ercole I d'Este. He invited her to come to Ferrara, more than two hundred miles away, where he pledged to build her a monastery. To the duke, Ferrara was becoming a center of the Renaissance, and he saw Lucy's presence as another step toward accomplishing that.

A two-year battle over where Lucy would live ensued before she left Viterbo for Ferrara in 1499. There, she found thirteen novices. When the new monastery was completed in 1501, it had space for more than a hundred women, which was very large for the time.

There is general agreement Lucy was not the best of superiors, and that a number of the novices (some personally selected by the duke's daughter-in-law, Lucrezia Borgia) and women religious sent from other monasteries were less than happy to be in Ferrara. But it is difficult to imagine the offense that would have justified in anyone's mind what followed.

Pope Alexander VI, who was also Lucrezia's father, died in 1503. Less than a month after his death, Lucy was ousted as superior in favor of Maria of Parma, a nun whom the pope had sent earlier in the year. Then in February 1505, a month after the duke's death, Lucy's life took an even more dramatic turn. She agreed in writing not to leave the convent that had been built for her, and to accept a new spiritual director who was unsympathetic to her charism. From that point on, Lucy would speak only to her spiritual director; if there were any need for private conversation, it had to be conducted in the presence of a designated sister. No longer would she be able to enter the convent parlor and interact with her sisters in casual conversation. Perhaps not surprisingly, she no longer experienced the stigmata. When she fell ill from time to time, she did not receive medical attention.

In 1544, her spiritual director asked Lucy to record her mystical experiences. She did so in a document called *Seven Revelations,* which describes Jesus, the Blessed Virgin, and St. Paul showing Lucy heaven. She died that same year, and with love, called the sisters to her and begged their forgiveness. When news of her death became known, people were shocked; they thought she had died much earlier. Her funeral had to be delayed because of the crush of those who wanted to attend.

It was not until 1710 that Lucy was beatified. Her *Seven Revelations* had been thought lost, but were discovered in 1999. They are full of vivid imagery, joy, and love.

LUCIA ON PERSECUTION:
(From a dialogue with Christ in *Seven Revelations:*) "Oil, dearest daughter, signifies the humility and meekness given to that soul and its action; and this is because oil humbles everything on which

it is placed, and is good for many things. It is a peaceful liquid, just as my soul was peaceful. I know how to suffer every evil and torment, as I did at the time of my Passion when I preached with all humanity."[8]

BRITISH WRITER LADY GEORGIANA CHARLOTTE FULLERTON ON LUCIA:
"When the last hour drew nigh, she called the sisters around her bed, and humbly asked their pardon for any scandal she had given them in life. We do not find one word of justification, or remonstrance, or even of regret; only some broken words of exhortation, not to be offended at her imperfection, but to love God and be detached from creatures, and abide steadfastly by their rule."[9]

REFLECTIONS FOR YOU:
- Is there someone in your life—your immediate or extended family, perhaps, or someone at the parish or work—who seems to dislike you for no reason? Consider humbling yourself by striking up a conversation about something you know this person enjoys or likes to talk about. Listen. Learn.
- It's easy to go along with the crowd, to gossip about or denigrate someone simply because other people do. Resolve that today, you will walk away from such conversations. Then do it again tomorrow and the next day.
- When Lucy passed away, people were surprised, because they thought she was already dead. Locate the address for a retired teacher, priest, or other person who had a positive influence on you but whom you haven't contacted in five or more years. Send a note of thanks, or say a prayer for that person's private intentions.

Learning More

You may be interested in learning more about persecution in the journeys of these women:

- Agnes Le Thi Thanh, 1781—July 12, 1841. Agnes and her Christian husband had six children and were devoted to their faith. She was arrested for hiding missionaries and allowing Masses to be held in their home. Agnes refused to trample on a crucifix or deny her faith despite three months of torture. She even rejected her husband's pleas that she renounce Christ for the sake of their family. She was the only laywoman in the group of 117 Martyrs of Vietnam who were canonized in 1988.

- Jeanne de Valois, April 23, 1464—February 4, 1505. Jeanne, the daughter of King Louis XI of France, was under no romantic illusions when at twelve she was married to a distant cousin, the Duke of Orleans. Marriages among royalty were always tied to politics. But she likely was surprised when, after twenty-two years of marriage, her husband assumed the throne after her brother's death and promptly sought to have their union annulled so he could marry her brother's widow. In humiliating detail, her husband publicly laid out his case, including his contention that Jeanne's physical deformities had prevented them from ever consummating the relationship. The annulment was granted on the questionable grounds that her father had forced her husband into the marriage. Jeanne said she would pray for him, and ultimately founded the Order of the Virgin Mary, a monastic congregation that aims to exemplify the Blessed Virgin's virtues. She was canonized in 1950.

- Zita of Lucca, c. 1218—1272. Zita went to work as a house servant for the wealthy Fatinelli family. Her industriousness—she was the first one up in the morning and did her chores with no complaints—and her piety—she walked fifteen miles to Mass in Pisa each day when the churches in Lucca had been ordered closed—did not sit well with the other servants or with the Fatinellis. She was mocked, reviled, even beaten. Through all this persecution, Zita just kept doing what the Lord wanted. Eventually, the others saw what a treasure she was, and she was promoted to head servant. She continued to treat all with kindness, and did not exact retribution over her former coworkers. Zita was canonized in 1696.

- Lillian and Natalie of Cordoba, died c. 852. The tension between Christians and Muslims was beginning to mount in Spain. Under Sharia law, it didn't matter which faith you wanted to follow; if your father was a follower of Islam, you were a follower of Islam. Aurelius found himself in that situation, married to Natalie, who was a convert. The couple practiced Christianity privately until the day Aurelius saw a Christian being scourged; they decided to go public, along with Aurelius's relative Felix and his wife, Lillian. Their open practice of Christianity, including visiting Christians in prison and the women going outside without their faces veiled, resulted in the foursome being among the more than forty people martyred by the Muslim government between 850 and 859 in Cordoba.

SUMMING IT UP AND TURNING IT OVER

Sára Salkaházi could have casually turned a corner and lived to battle another day against the Arrow Cross authorities' persecution. And yet, she didn't. Sára chose to say yes to offering herself up for righteousness. In a similar way, Laura Vicuña chose to be an oblation for her mother's immoral yet forgivable behavior.

Laura stood her moral ground, with support from the Salesian Sisters. And while the moments in which we suffer persecution may seem much smaller than these two, they really aren't. We diminish ourselves when we fail to stand for what is right, even at grave personal cost short of death, in the way that Mary of the Cross MacKillop did. Finally, there are times to offer up our agony and love our persecutors, as Lucy of Narni did.

Lord, guide me with the courage to speak forthrightly against persecution when you desire, and, when necessary, to bear it as you bore your cross.

Chapter Nine

JOY

"Rejoice and be glad, for your reward is great in heaven, for in the same way they persecuted the prophets who were before you."
—Matthew 5:12

As you read this book, you may have wondered about these women, and why each appears where she does. After all, Jeanne Jugan could have just as easily fit under Righteousness as under Spiritual Poverty. Maria Goretti certainly was persecuted. And you might think a few, such as Teresa of Calcutta and of course the Blessed Virgin, had lives that demonstrated aspects of all the Beatitudes.

That was my epiphany, my "aha" moment as I wrote this book and listened to the women's stories, those who lived thousands of years ago as well as the likes of those who breathed on earth during the same time I have: Chiara Badano, Gianna Beretta Molla, Teresa of Calcutta, Maria Quattrocchi, and Dorothy Day.

The Beatitudes are all the same.

Yes, you read that right.

The Beatitudes are all the same.

Each one of them calls for us to let go of the parts of ourselves that are displeasing to God and injurious to ourselves—fear, pride, greed, jealousy, and all the rest—today. Not after we think about it for a long time. Not after we put on our hair shirts and flog ourselves over what bad people we are for weeks on end. *Today.* That's why Jesus taught them in the present tense. So after much time spent making matrixes for the women and the Beatitudes, I realized there was an aspect of every woman's life that could have worked with each verse. I simply chose the one I felt, in prayer and meditation, would resonate the most with you.

Let me explain: If you are merciful, of course you hunger and thirst for righteousness and move closer to purity of heart. If you are a peacemaker, of course you understand and embrace the concepts of mercy and poverty of spirit that accompany listening to the views of those who wish you ill and respecting them as human beings. If you are obedient in your meekness to the Lord, of course you will be persecuted and reviled. And if you do any or all of these things, of course you will mourn. And also of course, you will find comfort—sometimes in your community; sometimes, surprisingly, in those who intended you harm; sometimes in yourself; and always, always, in God.

Every one of these sixty-four women and the thousands of other saints, blesseds, servants of God, and venerable who aren't here, men and women alike, knew the secret that the Beatitudes are all the same. They lived them. They suffered them. They celebrated them. Some of their crosses, like a spat in a convent or a spouse who smoked, may seem small to us; others, such as being murdered or forced into seclusion for decades on end, may seem unbearable. But they bore them with grace and, yes, joy and gladness once God showed them how to carry those crosses.

Not only are the Beatitudes all the same, our glorious saints, canonized and otherwise, are all the same too. They were people

who loved Christ even as they understood they would be persecuted here on earth, mindful and hopeful of that reward in heaven.
But that eventual reward wasn't all they thought about. Their
martyrdom and their heroic virtues show they were on fire to live
the life Jesus described on that mountain during their time here.

He desires no less from you.

CHAPTER ONE

1. Official site for the Postulation of the Cause for Canonization of Blessed Chiara Lubich, http://www.chiaralucebadano.it.

2. Official site for the Postulation of the Cause for Canonization of Blessed Chiara Lubich.

3. Faustina Kowalska, Divine Mercy in My Soul (Stockbridge, Mass.: Marian, 2005), p. 153.

4. "Faustina: Saint for the Third Millennium," Divine Mercy News, http://thedivinemercy.org/news/story.php?NID=3976.

5. "Servant, Nurse, Companion," Models of Holiness, *St. Anthony Messenger,* June 2007.

6. Sayings of Jeanne Jugan," Little Sisters of the Poor, http://www.littlesistersofthepoor.org/stjeannejugan/sayings-of-st-jugan.

7. OSV Newsweekly World Headlines, https://www.osv.com/OSVNewsweekly/RSS/RSSWorld/TabId/970/ArtMID/14185/ArticleID/3571/Future-saint-was-poor-in-goods-but-rich-in-faith.aspx, accessed February 6, 2015.

8. "St. Germaine Cousin," Catholic Online, http://www.catholic.org/saints/saint.php?saint_id=52.

9. "St. Germaine Cousin," St. Germaine Parish, http://www.stgermaineparish.org/about/st_germaine_cousin.html.

CHAPTER TWO

1. Fulton J. Sheen, *The Cross and the Beatitudes: Lessons on Love and Forgiveness* (Liguori, Mo.: Liguori, 2000), p. 87.

2. "Life and Affection," HL. Anna Schaffer, http://www.anna-schaeffer.de/biography.html.

3. "Spiritual Newsletter," Abbey of Saint-Joseph de Clairval, http://www.clairval.com/lettres/en/2003/02/02/2050203.htm.

4. Homily of His Holiness Pope Benedict XVI, October 21, 2012, http://www.vatican.va/holy_father/benedict_xvi/homilies/2012/documents/hf_ben-xvi_hom_20121021_canonizzazioni_en.html.

5. "Dear Friend of Saint Joseph Abbey," http://www.clairval.com/lettres/en/99/zb70499141298.htm.

6. "Dear Friend of Saint Joseph Abbey."

7. "Dear Friend of Saint Joseph Abbey."

8. "Dear Friend of Saint Joseph Abbey."

9. "Dear Friend of Saint Joseph Abbey."

10. Quoted in Ferdinand Holbock, *New Saints and Blessed of the Catholic Church:1979–1983,* vol. 1 (San Francisco: Ignatius, 2000), p. 79.

11. Quoted in Joseph I. Dirvin, *The Soul of Elizabeth Seton* (San Francisco: Ignatius, 1990), p. 57.

12. "Elizabeth Ann Seton Prayer Service," January 4, 2012, http://sisters-of-charity-federation.org/wordpress/wp-content/uploads/2011/12/EAS-Prayer-for-Jan-4pdf.

13. "Saint Louise De Marillac," http://www.catholicpamphlets.net/pamphlets/SAINT%20LOUISE%20DE%20MARILLAC.pdf.

14. "The Hands of Providence: Vincent de Paul, Louise de Marillac, and Feminine Charitable Activity in France, 1617-1660," *Vincentian Heritage Journal,* Volume 14, Issue 1, p. 64.

15. "Saint Louise De Marillac," http://www.catholicpamphlets.net/pamphlets/SAINT%20LOUISE%20DE%20MARILLAC.pdf.

CHAPTER THREE

1. Philip Schaff, *Leo the Great, Gregory the Great* (Christian Classics Ethereal Library) (n.p.: 1894), Sermon XCV, section V.

2. "Reflections of St. Gianna Beretta Molla," https://saintgianna.org/reflectionosst.htm.

3. Dr. Adrian Treloar, "Great Medical Lives: Blessed Gianna Molla," http://www.cmq.org.uk/CMQ/2012/May/blessed_gianna_molla.html.

4. Treloar.
5. Homily of His Holiness John Paul II, May 16, 2004.
6. "St. Pauline," http://fredsustik.com/StPauline.html.
7. "Paulina do Coração Agonizante de Jesus," http://www.vatican.va/news_services/liturgy/2002/documents/ns_lit_doc_20020519_paulina_en.html.
8. "Paulina do Coração Agonizante de Jesus."
9. "Paulina do Coração Agonizante de Jesus."
10. "Paulina do Coração Agonizante de Jesus."
11. Thérèse of Lisieux, *The Autobiography of Thérèse of Lisieux: The Story of a Soul* (Mineola, N.Y.: Dover, 2008), p. 2.
12. Thérèse of Lisieux, p. 5.
13. "Biography St Therese of Lisieux," http://www.biographyonline.net/spiritual/st_therese_lisieux.html
14. Thérèse of Lisieux, *Story of a Soul: The Autobiography of Thérèse of Lisieux*, Christian Classics Ethereal Library, n.d., n.p.
15. Guy Gaucher, *The Story of a Life: St. Theresa of Lisieux* (New York: HarperCollins, 1993), p. 219.
16. "Dear Friend of Saint Joseph Abbey," http://www.clairval.com/lettres/en/99/y31019920998.htm.
17. "The Message of Lourdes," http://en.lourdes-france.org/deepen/message-lourdes.
18. "St. Bernadette," http://www.catholic.org/saints/saint.php?saint_id=147.
19. Interview of the Holy Father Benedict XVI during the Flight to France, September 12, 2008.

CHAPTER FOUR

1. Father Daniel Ewald, *Saints and Blesseds of the Americas* (Bloomington, Ind.: Xlibris, 2009), p. 188.
2. "Homily for August 7, 2014," Fr. Warren's Homilies, http://fatherwarrencsb.blogspot.com/2014/08/homily-for-thursday-7-august-2014-ferial.html.

3. "Pope Francis celebrates Mass, proclaims new saints," Vatican Radio, http://en.radiovaticana.va/storico/2013/05/12/pope_francis_celebrates_mass%2C_proclaims_new_saints_(full_text)/en1-691365.

4. Hildegard Burjan, *A Conflicted Life,* p. 26, http://www.hildegardburjan.at/files/hb_vita_english.pdf.

5. Margarita Holzer, "Hildegard Burjan," http://www.unless-women.eu/biography-details/items/burjan.html.

6. "Blessed Maria Theresa Chiramel," http://www.missionariesoftheworld.org/2012/07/blessed-maria-theresa-chiramel.html.

7. Bosco Puthur, "Mariam Thresia: The Real Mother," http://mariamthresia.org/mariam-thresia-the-real-mother-bp-bosco-puthur/.

8. General Audience of His Holiness Benedict XVI, February 2, 2011.

9. Teresa of Avila, *The Collected Letters of Teresa of Avila,* vol. 2, trans. Kieran Kavanaugh, O.C.D., Otilio Rodriguez, O.C.D. (Washington, D.C.: ICS, 1976).

10. Cosmos Francesco Ruppi, "Honoring a Friendly and Firm 'Revolutionary for God,'" https://www.ewtn.com/library/MARY/teresavila.htm.

11. Shrine of St. Rose Philippine Duchesne, http://duchesneshrine.org/.

CHAPTER FIVE

1. "Questions and Answers," Nobel Prize, http://www.nobelprize.org/nobel_prizes/peace/laureates/1979/teresa-faq.html.

2. "Quotes Falsely Attributed to Mother Teresa," http://www.motherteresa.org/08_info/Quotesf.html.

3. "Mother Teresa of Calcutta (1910–1997)," http://www.vatican.va/news_services/liturgy/saints/ns_lit_doc_20031019_madre-teresa-en.html.

4. "Mother Teresa of Calcutta (1910–1997)."

5. Homily of John Paul II, Beatification of Maria Bernardina Jablonska and Mari Karlowska, June 6, 1997.

6. Homily of John Paul II, June 6, 1997.

7. "Not to the East, but to the West," Missionary Sisters of the Sacred Heart of Jesus, http://www.mothercabrini.org/who-we-are/our-history/not-to-the-east-but-to-the-west/.

8. Facebook, Cabrini Mission Corps, https://www.facebook.com/cabrini.mission.corps.fb/posts/10151587073177236. Accessed March 23, 2015.

9. Christopher Grosso, "Mother Cabrini the Eccentric?," https://cabrinimissionmatters.wordpress.com/2014/10/27/mother-cabrini-the-eccentric/

10. Elizabeth Canori Mora, *Life of the Venerable Elizabeth Canori Mora*, trans. Mary Elizabeth Herbert (Whitefish, Mt.: Kessinger, 2009), p. 46.

11. "Elisabetta Canori Mora," http://www.propheties.it/mystics/canori.htm.

12. Maria Elisabetta C.G. Mora, *Life of the Venerable Elizabeth Canori Mora*, p. 179.

13. Homily of His Holiness John Paul II, April 24, 1994. See also Ferdinand Holböck, *Married Saints and Blesseds: Through the Centuries* (San Francisco: Ignatius, 2002), p. 384.

CHAPTER SIX

1. Anthony Walton, "The Eye of the Needle: Katharine Drexel," http://magazine.nd.edu/news/10595-the-eye-of-the-needle-katharine-drexel/.

2. Cecilia Murray, "Katharine Drexel: Learning to Love the Poor," http://digitalcommons.lmu.edu/cgi/viewcontent.cgi?article=1346&context=ce.

3. Cheryl C.D. Hughes *Katharine Drexel: The Riches-to-Rags Story of an American Catholic Saint*, (Grand Rapids: Eerdmanns, 2014), p. 57.

4. "Cardinal Bevilacqua Celebrates Mass Honoring Feast Day of Blessed Katharine Drexel," http://archphila.org/press%20releases/pr000262.php.

5. "Beata Eurosia Fabris Barban," https://translate.google.com/translate?sl=auto&tl=en&js=y&prev=_t&hl=en&ie=UTF-8&u=www.eurosiafabrisbarban.it&edit-text=.
6. 'Catholic News Service, "'Extraordinarily ordinary' Italian mother was model of holiness," http://www.catholicnews.com/data/stories/cns/0506365.htm.
7. "St. Maria Goretti," http://www.catholicnewsagency.com/saint.php?n=530.
8. Message of His Holiness John Paul II to the Bishop of Albano for the Centenary of the Death of St. Maria Goretti, http://www.vatican.va/holy_father/john_paul_ii/speeches/2002/july/documents/hf_jp-ii_spe_20020708_santa-maria-goretti_en.html.
9. "The Revelations of the Two Hearts in Modern Times," http://www.ewtn.com/library/mary/firstsat.htm.
10. Mother Teresa, *Where There Is Love, There is God: Her Path to Closer Union with God and Greater Love for Others,* ed. Brian Kolodiejchuk M.C. (New York: Doubleday, 2012), p. 145.
11. "Quattrocchi (Blessed Luigi and Maria Beltrame)," Catholic Dictionary, http://dictionary.editme.com/Quattrocchi.

Chapter Seven
1. Augustine of Hippo, *Selections from Confessions and Other Essential Writings,* ed. Joseph T. Kelley (Woodstock, Vt.: Skylight Paths, 2010), p. 195.
2. Oscar Romero, *The Violence of Love,* ed. and trans. James R. Brockman (Farmington, Penn.: Bruderhof, 2003), p. 41, http://www.romerotrust.org.uk/documents/books/violenceoflove.pdf.
3. Dan Lynch, "Dorothy Day's Pro-Life Memories," http://www.catholiceducation.org/en/controversy/abortion/dorothy-day-s-pro-life-memories.html.
4. James Allaire, "Saint Therese of Lisieux inspired Dorothy Day," http://cjd.org/1996/06/01/saint-therese-of-lisieux-inspired-dorothy-day/.

5. "The Catholic Worker Movement," http://dorothydayguild.org/about-her-life/the-catholic-worker-movement/.
6. Cardinal John O'Connor, "Dorothy Day's Sainthood Cause Begins," http://www.catholicworker.org/dorothyday/canonizationtext.cfm?Number=82.
7. "Saint Josephine Bakhita, Universal Sister," Canossian Daughters of Charity, http://www.canossian.org/en/s-g-bakhita/.
8. "Josephine Bakhita: An African Saint," http://www.afrol.com/archive/josephine_bakhita.htm.
9. Benedict XVI, *Spe Salvi*, 48.
10. "Quotes by Saints," Archdiocese of Boston, http://www.boston-catholic.org/Being-Catholic/Content.aspx?id=11480.
11. General Audience of His Holiness Benedict XVI, November 24, 2010.
12. Maria J. Cirurgiao and Michael D. Hull, "Elizabeth of Portugal: 'For, in Her Is a Spirit Intelligent, Holy, Unique,'" http://www.ewtn.com/library/MARY/ELIZPORT.HTM.
13. Cirurgiao and Hull.

CHAPTER EIGHT
1. "Homily of Bishop László Biró," http://www.salkahazisara.com/beatif_en_homilia_kassa.html.
2. "'...the Kingdom of Heaven is Theirs...': Sr. Sara's Life in Mosaics," Blessed Sara Salkahazi sister of social service, http://www.salkahazisara.com/writings_en_mozaik.html.
3. "Saint Mary of the Cross MacKillop," The Catholic Church in Aotearoa New Zealand, http://www.catholic.org.nz/our-story/dsp-default.cfm?loadref=48.
4. Vigil Celebrating the Life of Mary Mackillop, October 16, 2010, Auditorium Conciliazione, Rome, http://www.marymackillop.org.au/_uploads/rsfil/000403_deab.pdf.
5. Cardinal George Pell, "Thanksgiving Mass for the Canonization of St. Mary of the Cross," October 18, 2010, http://www.sydneycatholic.org/people/archbishop/homilies/2010/20101019_1393.shtml.

6. "St. John Bosco," Bosconians Show What They've Got, http://boscoliva.webs.com/salesiansaints.htm.

7. John Cussen, "La Beata Laura Vicuña: The Nun's Version, Corrective of García Márquez's," http://www.academia.edu/9304848/La_Beata_Laura_Vicu%C3%B1a_The_Nun_s_Version_Corrective_of_Garc%C3%ADa_M%C3%A1rquez_s.

8. Thomas J. Heffernan and Thomas E. Burman, eds. *Scripture and Pluralism: Reading the Bible in the Religiously Plural Worlds of the Middle Ages and Renaissance* (Leiden: Koninklijke, 2005) p. 206.

9. J.M. Capes, *The Life of St. Frances of Rome,* http://www.gutenberg.org/cache/epub/8495/pg8495.html.

About the Author

Melanie Rigney is the author of *Sisterhood of Saints: Daily Guidance and Inspiration,* and a contributor to *Living Faith,* a 650,000-circulation Catholic devotional. She writes weekly for Your Daily Tripod, a Catholic blog, and has a monthly newsletter, "Sisters and Friends: Refresh Your Soul with Melanie Rigney." Rigney has spoken at the National Catholic Women's Conference, as well as several of their regional gatherings; numerous parishes, bookstores, and diocesan events; and several Theology on Tap sessions